THE SAGINAW PAUL BUNYAN

GREAT LAKES BOOKS

The SAGINAW ⸙PAUL⸙ BUNYAN

BY JAMES STEVENS

Woodcuts by
Richard Bennett

WAYNE STATE UNIVERSITY PRESS
DETROIT   1987

Manufactured in the United States of America.

91 90 89 88 87   5 4 3 2 1

Library of Congress Cataloging-in-Publication Data

Stevens, James, 1892–1971.
  The Saginaw Paul Bunyan / by James Stevens ; woodcuts by Richard Bennett.
         p.   cm. — (Great Lakes books)
  Reprint. Originally published: New York : Knopf, 1932.
  ISBN 0–8143–1929–7 (alk. paper). ISBN 0–8143–1930–0 (pbk. : alk. paper)
  1. Bunyan, Paul (Legendary character) I. Title. II. Series.
PS461.B8S83 1987
813'.52—dc19   87–24395
                                            CIP

To Theresa

CONTENTS

I

CONTENTS

II

THE SAGINAW PAUL BUNYAN

IN THE FIRST PLACE

PAUL BUNYAN is the unequaled hero of American out-door history. Whenever men of the woods circle a camp-fire, his famous name resounds. In their tales Paul is a bearded and mackinawed Hercules who moves mountains, tames rivers, subdues hurricanes, slays fearsome beasts, and, above all, rules men with incomparable humanity.

For Paul Bunyan is one hero of myth who kept kindness in his heart. This sublime quality makes him live on from the wastes of forgotten time, where selfish heroes have perished, or have achieved remembrance only as symbols of the monstrous forces that may be embodied in mankind.

Paul Bunyan owned the Lincoln spirit.

In all other respects the first and greatest of North Woods heroes revealed American traits in the grand style. When he began his incredible logging operations, Paul thought nothing of engaging a king as employment agent. Royalty meant little to the mighty woodsman. He rightly considered that a kind heart was more than a crown; so Paul Bunyan had no scruples whatever about looking a king straight in the eye and telling him to go to it.

That is figuratively speaking, of course. The bards who spin the history of Paul Bunyan around timberland campfires are emphatic to the point of profanity in declaring that the great logger never set foot on Europe's shore or matched stares with a living king. These spinners of history all agree that Paul rose to power in the Quebec country during the winter of the Blue Snow, acquired his roguish and rugged ox, Babe, in the same portentous season, and in his own good time invented logging as the mightiest occupation a woodsman could know. From Quebec Paul Bunyan logged up Big Auger River and then won his supreme fame in the Saginaw timber country.

Not once did the free-hearted hero point his beard toward royalty-ridden Europe. Nevertheless, he sent an order by air to the boss King.

A carrier eagle bore the order over the ocean wastes. Without any pious nonsense, the order read for the King to gather up enough men to log off the old Saginaw. While the monarch took the order, the American carrier eagle looked him straight in the eye. The eagle did this as proxy for Paul Bunyan, to show the King what freedom, independence, and kindness were like.

The boss King himself did not stand on ceremony. Europe at that time—it was a time far beyond our count and is thus ignored in documented and chronologized history—was overrun with many wild varieties of men. The King seized the opportunity to get rid of a host of the wildest, and devoted every royal energy to the grave and difficult matter. Soon this sign was swinging hugely from the palace front:

PETE BARNUM
EMPLOYMENT AGENT FOR PAUL BUNYAN

In his spare time
Pete the First
King of Europe.

So Paul Bunyan got his Wild Irish, Terrible Swede, Hairy Scotch, and Fighting French varieties of men. He culled them lavishly, and from the residue fashioned the mightiest lumberjack crew of timber-country history. These were the first shanty boys of the North Woods. All had hair on their chests and the old fight in their eyes. The least of them could send six shirt-buttons popping with one deep breath.

At last the boss logger of the North Woods was ready to invade the Saginaw. The jacks were packed in the shanties, and these were anchored to the serpentine sled. Babe the Blue Ox was yoked and hitched. Paul Bunyan faced the southwest. Johnny Inkslinger, the tremendous timekeeper, and Hels Helson, formidable foreman, took their posts.

The start was simply made. Quebec fell rapidly behind. The wilderness waited.

Until the emptying basin of Big Auger River was reached, the journey was devoid of interest. In the meantime the occasion is good for the historian's customary note of personal explanation.

The earnest seeker amid the plain facts of history is never satisfied by twice told tales. He dutifully reads what better men have written, but his mightiest urge is to poke and pry on his own hook in original sources. A kindred impulse moves the seeker in the kind of history that is too old to be documented. This was the spirit that fetched me to the Saginaw Valley of Michigan, in an endless hunt for original accounts of the conquests and labors of Paul Bunyan.

I was a Western woodsman. In the foggy fir forests of the Pacific slope and in the glamorous pine lands of the Cascades I had heard the deeds of the king jack of all loggers recited for nigh on twenty-five years. By the time the down on my chest had grown into a harsh and tawny stubble I myself was fledging into a camp bard. In summer nights by the smudge fire and in winter nights by the bunkhouse heater I revised the tales of older bards, giving them whatever form the inspiration of the moment revealed.

For this is the one royal road to truth in the history of Paul Bunyan. It has no documents for the seeker. Truth comes to the Bunyan bard as it comes to the Gospel preacher, in flashes of inspiration. There is a body of simple texts known to all woodsmen. Here is one of them:

"Paul Bunyan invented logging in the winter of the Blue Snow."

The honest bard never repeats the tale another has told about the famous season. He takes his text, lets the Bunyan spirit work, and then tries to *cast new light*, as the loggers say, on the first grand event of timber-country history.

Long after my ordination in the woods, I recorded certain elements of the history of Paul Bunyan in a book. I kept the pious purpose and followed the sacred method of the old camp bards in this work, never repeating another's tale, but yielding entirely to inspiration. Often the light failed, but some new facts were revealed.

Never relaxing my efforts in the search for bigger and better truths, I eventually embarked for the homeland of the first and best of all boss loggers.

This land is the lower peninsula of Michigan, which lies like a mitten on the map. The thumb juts eastward into Lake Huron, opening for the gap of Saginaw Bay. Into the bay flows the most celebrated of lumber rivers. This stream also bears the great name Saginaw.

In the years from 1850 to 1900 twenty-five million acres of pine were harvested off the lands between Saginaw Valley and the northern shore of the upper peninsula. In that time lumbering was a primitive industry. Choppers, swampers, and teamsters went into the wilderness each autumn. The camps were rude log shanties. The pine logs were hauled to the rivers on sleighs and stacked in enormous banks during the winter months. With the bursting of spring freshets, the rollways were broken and the logs driven down to the mills.

Then the lumber towns roared. Bay City alone had two hundred and sixty-five saloons in the mid eighties. The lumberjacks—the term "logger" is applied to the axman only in the Far West—were like soldiers unloosed from the wars. For long months they had lived hard and dangerously in the wilderness. The life refused men who were not brawny and bold. Now the jacks had money in their pockets and were free to realize their winter dreams of a season of "good old times."

The times of revelry in the shacks about the sawdust piles of the river towns were rowdy and wild, but they were never good. Yet the old dreams would glitter up again as soon as the jacks had returned to the pineries. They always came back, though damning their hardships and dangers. The true woodsmen could never quit the camps. They followed the lumbermen west.

The old timber country is now a waste of sand plains. The pineries live only in the recitations of the gnarled and withered jacks who survive. From them I learned a vast number of new truths concerning the early history of the mightiest and kindest of boss loggers. But I am still not the one to break the main law and tell tales twice. All the famous facts about the Saginaw are in this book, but upon them I cast my own light, thus observing the obligations of tradition.

Paul Bunyan was not the discoverer of the great timber country. There were already heroes in the foreground when the boss logger started his march from Quebec.

The mightiest was the invulnerable and irresistible iron man of the Saginaw, Shot Gunderson. The slyest and cutest was Squatter John, who was grabbing cornland below the southern border. The most secretive and the one most perilous to Paul Bunyan was the rover of the Seven Mississippis, Joe Le Mufraw.

The wilderness waited in the Saginaw for Paul Bunyan, and so did war.

The grand wild country itself was entirely surrounded by running water when the boss logger started on his trip. Its peninsula days were yet to come. Round River, the Father of Waters, flowed ceaselessly and with inconceivable majesty about the land. There were two outlets from the great circle. In the north Round River drove an arm through a range of iron mountains. This arm spread into the Seven Mississippis, which flowed west, side by side, through a great plain. From the southern bend the Big Auger twisted and tossed, boring northeastward to Quebec and the sea.

At last Paul Bunyan led his train along the rim of the Big Auger's emptying basin. The red glow of an autumn sunset faded behind darkening pines. The jacks stared eagerly from the doors of swaying and heaving shanties. They were watching for signs of the Year of Good Old Times to appear. King Pete had promised that the prophesied year would shine down before long in the Saginaw alone.

"She's a weary fall and winter yet," warned the wisest jacks. "Hold yer hosses there. Get set to stop and stretch legs. The Big Feller [1] is slowin' Babe down."

Paul Bunyan was indeed ordering the Blue Ox to halt. Just ahead the Big Auger foamed from its spiral gorge.

The invasion of the Saginaw timber country had begun.

[1] Michigan woodsmen termed any lumberman who employed them "the Old Feller." So Paul Bunyan, first and greatest of the tribe of boss loggers, was "the Big Feller" to his men.

I

THE OUTPOST OF THE SAGINAW

BABE THE BLUE OX hauled up before a cliff which bulked seventy-one ax-handles high. Babe was weary from the long drag through mud made by autumn rains, and he rested his chin on the cliff top. The lids sank over his bulging eyes like purple clouds descending over two blue moons. His flanks heaved in peaceful sighs as Hels Helson unhitched and unyoked him. Babe drowsed in the eventide.

To the rear the serpentine tote sled, loaded with bunk shanties and stores, let its smoking runners cool and settled for the night. The shanty boys piled out to stretch their legs, which were always kinked unmercifully in the rides they endured behind the bounding Blue Ox. To stretch their legs properly, the jacks solemnly hung by their heels from the lower boughs of convenient pines. Not one of them dreamed that this common observance of established custom presaged disaster.

Nor did the scene presage anything of the sort to Paul Bunyan. This form of leg-stretching was one of his favorite inventions. When moving camp, it had always irked the boss logger to regard the futility of the feeble leg-stretching methods in vogue among his men. After a stiff day's ride they would hobble about, kicking out clownishly with their right feet, then with their left ones, seldom obtaining relief. So Paul had invented hanging by the heels to baffle the kinks, and thereafter the stiffest among the men could stretch his legs thoroughly in jig time.

The shanty boys were so used to their Big Feller's invention by now that they all filled and lit their pipes as they swung in this kind eventide. Heels up, head down, every jack puffed contentedly while Paul Bunyan prepared to commend himself and his men to the Big Auger as goodwill ambassadors.

He was too late. Hels Helson, the Big Swede, had perched by Babe's head to remove a troublesome tree from his boot. It was a jack pine no more than nine feet long, but it was thorny and had worked down to his heel, irritating the hide. Hels pulled off the boot and shook it. The pine failed to fall out. Hels next turned the top of the boot toward the setting sun, to get some light into his subject, and then he saw the river.

For a long minute Hels gaped and blinked, unable to believe his eyes. Then his jaws began to get set for a laugh. Like brainier men, the Big Swede would either scowl or laugh at anything he did not understand. The Big Auger was beyond him. This time his lack of understanding put an edge on his ribs. Hels set himself for a rousing guffaw.

That was a signal for powerful trouble to hustle up.

The Big Auger was wild, young, and proud. Unassisted, the river had bored out a bed for itself from the southeastern bend of the great Round. Having won independence, the Big Auger owned an umbrageous American pride in its prowess. From the parent river to its emptying basin the young stream foamed and roared proudly in every inch of its course. Its flowing style was all its own. The body of the Big Auger was a monster moving spiral in a hard rock bed. The banks were strewn with rock shavings. Only screwfish lived in the perpetually twisting waters. The one branch of the Big Auger was the Little Gimlet. The fork of the two streams was the eastern outpost of the Saginaw timber country.

The Big Auger was not unique in a wilderness where nature was yet in emergence from prehistoric disorder. The river was simply strange to Hels Helson.

For that long moment the Big Swede gaped incredulously at the twisting flow of the stream, with its spiral channels a steely blue, the swirling ridges between the channels glittering like curved sword blades, all tossing darts of spray and spears of foam. For that moment Hels stared; then his jaws began to spread. His Adam's apple clicked in a convulsive bob. Hels grinned—he chuckled—

"Bay yee, this river har has got its tail twisted yust like Ay twist the Blue Ox tail ven Ay vant play gude yoke on Babe. Hey, you fool river, you! Who twist yoor tail, noo?"

When the Big Swede got a joke on anybody, he gave it every laugh he had. Now he held his ribs and roared.

The Big Auger also roared. It was offended intolerably by this foreigner's laugh at its grandest matter of pride. The river did not know, of course, that Hels Helson had imagined that some mighty power was twisting its tail. The river only realized that its strange flow had aroused snorts of ridicule. So the Big Auger roared wrathfully out of its bed and drove with full force for the gaping mouth of Hels Helson, which yawned like a mammoth cave as he held his sides and snorted.

Just in the nick of time Hels Helson saw the rampageous river striking at him like a gigantic blue and white snake. He hurled his boot with a frantic swing. Luckily for him, the flapping boot-top met the Big Auger head on and smothered it for an instant. The river furiously shook the boot off, hurling it high and far. The hurtling boot ripped a cloud into tatters, ravaging the beauty of the sunset. Then it sailed on with a thunderous hissing whine for the horizon, sprinkling the pines as it sailed.

In the meanwhile Hels had ducked below the cliff and charged for safety in a stooping run. All might have gone well with him had not Babe been awakened by the turmoil and, obedient to his regular waking habit, carelessly swung out his tail in a lazy switch to the right.

The brush of Babe's tail struck Hels squarely on the neck. Then it coiled into a loop before his eyes. The Big Swede could not stop soon enough. He plunged into the loop, and Babe's tail jerked into a tight half hitch about his neck. Panic smote Hels Helson now. He imagined the river had seized him, with the object of choking him down. He charged for the hills in a wild frenzy. A violent uproar to the rear goaded Hels on.

The uproar was actually the agonized bellow of Babe. Hels Helson was unwittingly turning the tables on the Blue Ox. Ordinarily it was Babe who dragged the formidable foreman, heaving and bouncing Hels on the way to work in the woods. But nothing could now halt the Big Swede's plunging gallop to the hills. Babe pawed dirt and bellowed, but his tail was solidly caught; and at last the Blue Ox gave up and galloped backward, his great blue eyes bulging in mute appeal at Paul Bunyan.

All this had happened in little more than an instant, as actions not only speak louder than words, but move incomparably faster. In the next instant, just as Paul wheeled about to rescue Babe, a second disaster fell.

The earth quaked from the thunder of the galloping ox and foreman; and this quaking, by the operation of a natural law, was transmitted to the pines that flanked the tote sled. The heels of every suspended jack were jerked from his bough, and the entire host dropped, head first, as one man. The forest floor was spongy from autumn rains, and every jack plunged in shoulders-deep. All appeared to be solidly stuck in the mud. Under every tree legs pumped so furiously and boots tossed with such violence that the shanty boys seemed to be trying to jig while standing on their heads.

The instant passed. Then, as Paul Bunyan wheeled once more, this time to rescue his men, the Big Auger, trembling with outraged pride, determined to punish somebody, squirted seventy-nine barrels of water into the eye of the majestic boss logger of the North Woods!

In three instants three major disasters had fallen on Paul Bunyan. And as yet he had not even entered the Saginaw country. Small wonder that he felt a shadow creep over his faith in the future as he poked with his behemoth bandanna and swabbed out the corner of his eye in which the river water had gathered.

"Three blasted disasters to retrieve," murmured the boss logger glumly. "Mightly likely it'll take all winter."

The Big Auger knew what it had done. Under the injured and reproving glance of the boss logger of the North Woods the wild young river dropped back into its bed. Now a mutter sounded as an undertone to its defiant roar. That mutter was the voice of fear.

The Big Auger was still master of the situation, however, and waited defiantly for Paul Bunyan's next move.

That move of course was to reorganize the forces. Pocketing his behemoth bandanna, Paul Bunyan turned his back on the river and strode to the rescue of his shanty boys. The river heaved with relief and swelled with pride. It seemed to think that it had already won the battle. But the Big Auger little knew Paul Bunyan. He had not yet begun to fight.

The rescue of the shanty boys was characteristic of their Big Feller. It was plain to him that in pulling the disaster victims from the mire one by one so much time would be used that the last men reached would suffocate before the rescue. Already many legs were kicking in slow motion. Every move served only to immerse the men's heads deeper in the mud. Some were mired to their belts. The arms of every man were held tightly to his sides. Fingers drooped feebly. Booted feet sagged down.

Paul Bunyan did not hesitate. A simple means of instant rescue flashed into his brain. If it worked, he could save one hundred and eleven men at a lick instead of one. His hands swept down to make the test.

Instead of plucking men from the mud, Paul Bunyan plucked pines. From each tree an average of one hundred and eleven men had been hanging by the heels in the ceremony of leg-stretching. About the roots of each tree legs stuck up like tenpins. Now the boss logger's logic proved itself. The first pine plucked and tossed aside left its entire quota of shanty boys kicking and squirming in the rents of the torn earth. They wheezed mud and pawed it from their noses and eyes, but they were safe. Paul's boots swung over them with a high clearance, and another pine was plucked and tossed. Paul Bunyan went down one row of pines and up the other like a farmer uprooting potato vines, only he unearthed shanty boys.

The men themselves took this view of the situation.

' The Big Feller shorely leave us feelin' like small potaters," they wheezed, when nearly all were out.

So that celebrated wheeze got its start.

As the last gang was safely disinterred, Paul Bunyan surveyed the scene, at the same time brushing his hands. The mode of action had worked. The few men who had not come up with the pine roots were being rescued by their mates. Soon all were up and brushing whiskers.

One disaster was retrieved. Paul Bunyan was ready for the other two.

"Set up the cook shanty there," he roared. "Here we make our start! We're going to show this river here how to get out the logs, by the slivery cedars of the old Lebanon!"

The shanty boys grinned through the mud that still stuck to their mustaches. This was the kind of talk they wanted to hear! Nobody thought now of the Year of the Good Old Times. A bully timber fight loomed ahead.

The jacks cocked their ears in the hollows of their hands. They listened to the river. The Big Auger was ready to fight. There was a menacing snarl in its defiant roar.

"Sounds mighty bad." The shanty boys dubiously shook their heads. "No fightin' wolf like a skeered one. And this here Big Auger is shore a wolf among rivers. We got a bad battle comin' up."

Paul Bunyan now took to the hills, following the trail of Babe and Hels. It was winding and long. Paul strode on, into the sunset, met and passed twilight, and finally faced a rising full moon. Here he saw signs along the trail that indicated a slackening in the runaway gallop of the Big Swede.

First, the track left by Hels's one bare foot was not in evidence for a mile. On the other hand, or, rather, foot, the unmated boot track was deeper here. It was plain that Hels had made this mile by hopping. Next, two ragged strips of cloth were illumined in the trail by the inquisitive round moon. Paul paused to examine the strips. It took him no time at all to decide that they were important integers of the Big Swede's breeches.

Certain marks on the cloth strips showed them to be from the seat. Paul Bunyan never mistook sitting-down marks. Some bigger and fresher marks had obviously been made by snapping teeth. Paul paused now to deduce. He soon reached the conclusion that Babe had snapped these cloth strips from the rear of Hels. Deducing further, it was plain to Paul Bunyan that the Big Swede had slowed down to a pace which permitted Babe, though galloping backward, to gain the distance needed for twisting his head and indulging in a bite.

Paul Bunyan sighed with relief and proceeded with certainty. He had never heard of such a variety of man as the detective, but the boss logger was a great specimen of the species, none the less.

Consequently he was not astonished by the spectacle that met his eyes at dawn. Paul Bunyan had already deduced it. Tramping over a piny hump, he first saw a broad plain from which a seemingly boundless body of water extended. Then his vision was focused on the spectacle of Babe and Hels.

The unfortunate foreman was standing on his booted foot, while the other was drawn up under himself. His head hung dejectedly. In the gray dawn light Hels looked like a huge sorrowful crane. Two bare spots surrounded by jagged edges of breeches cloth further affirmed the accuracy of Paul Bunyan's detective work. Now Hels was extending his right hand in a gesture of supplication. The foreman's voice sounded prayerfully.

"Oh, bay yee, Ay like you, Babe! Ay vas alvays gude feller to you, Babe! Ay vish you vould be so gude to me and give may boot back noo!"

Paul felt a throb of joy as he saw that the Big Swede's lost boot was dangling from Babe's teeth. An artesian well spouting from the plain showed where the boot had struck. Luck was smiling a little. Providing new boots for Hels was ever an arduous business. The hide of a whale was required for the uppers alone. Now Paul Bunyan would not need to go whaling for shoe leather.

Babe was keeping possession of the found boot and teasing the foreman. Hels, as usual, was taking the play of the Blue Ox with extreme seriousness. Babe stiffened his forelegs toward Hels, crouched down on them, his tail switching joyously from his elevated rear, his head turned sidewise with the boot, while he twitched his ears and rolled his eyes roguishly at the supplicating Swede. Paul Bunyan chuckled through his beard at that, but Hels groaned anew.

"Har noo, Babe," he pleaded. "Coom har vit' may boot noo, like gude feller."

He hopped for the Blue Ox. Babe's tail switched on. Another hop—and just as Hels grabbed for the boot, Babe snorted, wheeled about on his hind legs, loped for rods, then resumed his former position.

"Noo, bay yee, Ay vas mad!" roared the Big Swede.

Still roaring, he pitched into a blind headlong charge for the Blue Ox. Now Babe played on Hels the most heartless trick of all. He capered on, heading directly for the artesian well. Bounding over it, he naturally smothered the spouting water, and Hels did not see it until too late. Just as he grabbed for Babe's tail, the artesian fountain was freed again. Bursting out behind the ox, it roared and foamed up the open breeches leg of the Big Swede and spouted out of his shirt-collar. Hels fought the geyser madly for a moment, then collapsed.

The prospect of a washing was always the most dreadful one Hels Helson could face. He could bear the ordeal only once a year. Last spring he had labored through a tremendous one. Here it was only early autumn. No wonder Hels had run from the Big Auger in a mad panic and blind frenzy. No wonder he collapsed after a short, fierce tussle with the artesian well.

It was simply too much. After his long and painful run from the river he had been washed anyhow. For once in his life rough and gruff Hels Helson was about to blubber. But Paul Bunyan saved him from that shame.

"Enough, Babe!" commanded the boss logger sternly. "Fetch Hels his boot here."

The Blue Ox instantly sobered up and submitted. All his sportiveness was shed. His tail drooped between his hind legs and he approached Hels in a humble and contrite manner. He dropped the boot in the foreman's lap, he protruded his moist tongue and gave the unfortunate's neck a couple of consoling licks, then he rolled his eyes at Paul Bunyan, begging mutely for forgiveness.

Forgiveness was of course freely bestowed. The boss logger was never one to cry over spilled ink or to reproach the spiller; he always proceeded at once to wipe out the spots. Paul Bunyan wasted no time now. His most courageous tone boomed from his beard.

"She's boots and axes for us, Hels! Lace up and make ready to swing. We're not moving for the Round River crossing yet. First we're logging off Big Auger Valley, then we're taming down that curly wolf of a river for a drive. Hustle, Hels!"

Paul Bunyan made the last two words sound like the whistling whine of a thousand ax-blades hurtling through the frosty air. Both the Blue Ox and the Big Swede at once came to earnest attention. There would be no more frolics until spring. It was hard labor now, hard labor and bully battle. The boss logger of the North Woods had given the word, and his word was law.

Not once did Paul Bunyan look behind him as he started the return march from the plain. He knew that the apparently boundless body of running water was actually Round River. Beyond the flow of its endless tide lay the old Saginaw. The wilderness waited. But Paul Bunyan turned his back on it here and now.

There was work to do and war to be made at the outpost of the Saginaw. The Big Auger had flung its challenge into Paul Bunyan's eye. That challenge must be met.

II

TAMING OF THE BIG AUGER

A CAMP was made below the fork of the Little Gimlet. Choppers, swampers, and road-builders were dispersed throughout the tremendous triangle of timberland that undulated over the hills and flattened in the plain that fringed the Round. Skid trails for the Blue Ox were chopped and swamped out. Babe was such a monster of a skidder that only thin lines of timber were left standing when the trails were cleared for him. Heaps of logs grew into piles, these flourished into hills, and with the first snowfall mountains of pine timbers bulked in all the trails.

The axes were exchanged for peaveys. The jacks swarmed to the banking-grounds. Hels Helson hitched Babe to the first mountain of logs. The Blue Ox bellied down. Pine Mountain Number One moved over the frozen snow to the snarling river.

The boss logger of the North Woods marched before it there. His tread was harsh and firm, and the glitter of purpose in his eyes was like that of frosty steel in the hard winter sunlight. On the bank of the defiant river the jacks bated their breath and stared with unblinking eyes. For the first time since King Pete had shipped them over, the men made a human scene which stirred Paul Bunyan. Against the sullen gray of the foaming river, the whiteness of the far bank, the black boles of the pines beyond, canopied by snowy boughs gleaming with frost crystals, the jacks were fiery figures. Red mackinaw checks blazed there, and so did scarlet Quebec sashes and caps. From mittened hands gleamed the polished steel of peavey prongs and spears. The brawny and fiery human scene inspired Paul Bunyan.

"Let the Big Auger be as rambunctious, rampageous, and rotary as it wants to be," growled the boss logger in his beard, "but it's never going to beat me before my men. Not no more than the Flood beat Noah, by the cubits of the old ark!"

The river roared. Ever and on its snarling defiance boomed sullenly under the bluish pallor of the sky and through the white woods. Paul Bunyan paid the roar no mind, beyond keeping a vigilant and purposeful eye on the Big Auger's flow.

The Blue Ox wheeled on the banking-grounds. He halted in position, and at a low word from Paul Bunyan the peavey men leaped to labor. Pine Mountain Number One thundered into place on the rollways. Before the last crash had echoed through the woods, the river looped up from its bed, obviously with the intention of raking the banked logs down to destruction. In minutes the pine sticks would be whirled and pounded into splinters.

Paul Bunyan was ready. With a backhanded lick he

struck the looping river squarely in its middle and batted it down into the grooved bed of hard rock. The Big Auger subsided with a watery moan.

"That took the curl out of its tail!" yelled the delighted jacks.

Paul Bunyan shrewdly shook his head.

"A river like that one don't lay down for a single lick," he said. "Something fishy in it. Speaking of fish, just you remember not to count your trout before they're catched."

With that cryptic remark, the boss logger returned to the woods. The shanty boys figured that for once their Big Feller was wrong. The Big Auger let the day go on and the logs pile up without another threatening throw, with never another defiant roar. The jacks were jubilant as they returned to camp.

"Got the old river goin'," they declared. "Time spring busts fer the drive, it'll be runnin' smooth as a ribbon."

Paul Bunyan, however, kept one eye and an ear open all that night. Just before dawn he started up at a rising roar from the river. Seven strides took him down the trail. A splintering crash of timbers shattered the dawn. Paul Bunyan rolled up his sleeves and heaved down to save his logs. His last scruples against using force on the wild young stream were gone. The Big Auger had rejected all overtures of peace. It had to be war.

Paul Bunyan's war plans were already prepared. He made directly for the fork of the Little Gimlet. Here seven sizable hills bulged between the two streams. One by one, Paul scooped them up and pitched them

into the Big Auger. In no more than nineteen minutes
the fighting river was damned from brim to brim. The
hills were solid rock. Tamped down, they formed a
powerful barrier. Against the wall the river heaved and
surged, rolling in mamouth waves, tossing clouds of
spray that froze and showered icicles as far as the camp.

"There you'll stay till you're untwisted and tamed,"
said the boss logger, with grim brevity. "Faunch all you
blasted please. You're a tied-up river."

He then brushed his hands, buttoned his collar, and
serenely returned to call his men to labor.

In a month it appeared that the Big Auger was truly
tamed and regretted its night attack on the log banks.
Day by day the wrath of its waters subsided, until at
last the river lay like a calm lake behind the dam of
solid rock hills. On the first night of spring the Big
Auger seemed to repose with the placidity of a pasture
pond.

Paul Bunyan, always ready to trust and forgive,
smiled through his beard at the subdued young river.
For the first time he ventured to pet the Big Auger,
reaching down with his great hand, stroking the river,
whispering soothing words.

"Let's be kind friends," said Paul Bunyan. "Let's be,
now."

The Big Auger seemed to wag its tail, and the boss
logger was thereby lulled into a false sense of security
at last. He was weary from the winter of logging, and he
wanted at least one night's rest before opening the dam
for the drive. So he nodded in his first sleep since

sight. Then he observed the fear of the shanty boys, and doubt clouded the eyes of the good ox. Now Babe's moo warned the river not to go too far in this rough sport. Hels Helson stood in perplexity, imagining that the boss logger was simply taking a new kind of spring bath. Johnny Inkslinger, always a devotee of figures, kept pencils going like mad as he checked the number of Mr. Bunyan's rotations per minute.

The lowering clouds formed by tatters of mackinaw, breeches, red underwear, and green socks still hovered over the battle scene. The shaggy boughs of bull pines dripped from the morning mist. It was a fitting atmosphere for a solemn and awful fray.

The Big Auger was losing its twist in the relentless grip of Paul Bunyan. Now the river gathered all its powers for one desperate effort to shake itself free. It took to the air again, spiraling in enormous twists and turns, but the throttling and scissoring grip of the boss logger of the North Woods held true. The Big Auger heaved and surged into the climax of its mightiest battle thrust.

All its powers, from source to mouth, were gathered and unloosed. There was an appalling convulsion of waters, from which the body of the Big Auger bucked up until it was a gigantic loop, with the hump parting the artificial clouds.

The patches and tatters of clouds rolled back and began to fall in threads. The shanty boys brushed off this wool rain and stared breathlessly into the golden burst of sunlight that played on the climax of the battle. Up and up the river humped itself and swelled, shaking in a truly towering rage. High on the hump the Big Feller was rotated with such speed that the friction made the water boil. Scalding drops showered down. Steam spouted nine ways. The shanty boys breathed a prayer.

"Oh, lordy, if the river only don't scald through the Big Feller's hide!" they prayed.

Their prayer was in vain. High up on the riotous hump of the bucking river Paul Bunyan suddenly quivered, stiffened, and yelled in the motions and tone used only by a man when he is scalded, blistered, scorched, singed, or sizzled. It looked and sounded like a hot licking for the Big Feller.

The heat, however, had burned two ways. The nine clouds of condensed steam spouting from the Big Auger meant that the river was thinning down. Then, when Paul Bunyan jerked and stiffened convulsively from the percolations through his hide, his clamped legs sheared through the thinned body of hard water like a lightning stroke. It was the beginning of the end.

The hump parted, and the Big Auger collapsed in two boiling and hissing sections. Between them Paul Bunyan thundered down, his hide smoking. Like any trained riverman, he instinctively lit on his feet. No fall could break him when he lit on them. Paul Bunyan bounced three times; then he too collapsed between the boiling lakes.

Like dead the cooling halves of the sundered river lay for three days and nights. Paul Bunyan lay like a dead man through the same period. When he recovered his strength and wits, the Big Auger was also recovering, flowing on in a lukewarm fashion. Its surface was smooth and fair. The river rampaged, roared, and rotated no more. The boss logger turned toward his camp.

"All out for the drive there!" he commanded, a ringing tone of triumph subduing the weariness in his voice. "We've made a pious lumber river out of the Big Auger, by the old Deuteronomy! We take the drive down, and then, by the old Exodus, we head on for the Saginaw!"

The drive was taken down without a bobble. Never again was the Big Auger that in fact as well as in name. But Paul Bunyan gave the river a monument by which it could always remember its proud and independent youth. Where the Big Auger had bored through the seven hills, there was now a grand waterfall. That was left in peace. Later its name was vulgarized into Niagara.

Yet another fine form of life followed Paul Bunyan up Big Auger River. In this same spring schools of whales used the tamed stream as a route to Round River, which the leviathans regarded as ideal for calving-grounds and nursing-waters. Until the spring of the Mud Rain whale calves enjoyed the circular Father of Waters as a merry-go-round perfectly suited to their natures.

But this is a matter of botany which must be reserved for a botanical chapter. History still claims attention. Its next demand is an account of Paul Bunyan's calamitous crossing of Round River and his portentous entrance into the Saginaw timber country.

III

THE ROUND RIVER CROSSING

THE weather was at its kindest when Paul Bunyan struck Round River. The time of his crossing over the Father of Waters is remembered as the Year of the Lost Summer. Spring replaced the mislaid season, blossoming and smiling on until autumn. The bluest of rain-washed skies arched above Round River the morning the crossing was started. The sunshine was sweet gold. From the trail behind the speeding camp, breezes blew smells of crushed buds and grass along. Ahead the river smiled.

As always, Paul Bunyan led the van. Attaching right and left water plows to his shins, he struck into the shining waters with a steady stride. A hand shading his eyes, the boss logger sighted an imaginary line for the lone landmark, a rugged brown peak bulging through the soft horizon haze. That line should be held until the unseen far bank was reached.

Paul Bunyan had no doubts. The river bottom was hard. Never yet had he encountered a river too deep for his water plows. It never occurred to Paul that he might have to swim in this one. He waded confidently on. Only once did he turn his head. That was to imbue the jacks with his own confidence.

He said nothing, only smiling kindly through his beard. Then his hand swung up, over and on toward the unseen Saginaw, in the most reassuring of highball signs. Even the shanty boys who were the most pop-eyed and the palest around the gills were cheered, and responded with sickly grins. The bulliest roared.

"Let 'er go galliger, Big Feller!" they roared. "We don't know where, but we're on our way! Any old place we hang our hats is sweet home to us! Hard to lose and too tough to kill!"

"Getting to be real jacks, men are," murmured the boss logger with pride. "Hair on their chests and the old fight in their eyes! Yay, Babe!"

For three hours and more Paul Bunyan easily thrust into the majestic stream. His driving legs plowed the waters, and behind him Johnny Inkslinger, Hels Helson, and Babe the Blue Ox tramped on a dry river bed. On each side of the trail parted by Paul a monster wave rolled up and away from a plowshare. Before these waves could halt, recede, and merge again, the serpentine sled had been skidded on. There was plenty of dry land to spare in the wake of the speeding camp.

The famous tote sled got its name from being built like a joint snake. Each camp building had a pair of steel-shod skids for itself. When all were coupled together and Babe was hitched and speeded up, the whole rig would glide over all obstacles like a giant serpent. The Blue Ox traveled so fast that the friction of the runners would burn the earth into a slick, glassy track.

The larger buildings, such as Babe's ten-acre stable, headed the grand rig. The shanties followed. At the tail was Hels Helson's sled of snoose. This mineral was the prime necessity of the Big Swede's life. As a panacea the only equal of snoose known to history is pantagruelion, the celebrated herb of France. The difficulty with snoose was that it was too explosive to be used by any creature in camp besides Hels Helson. For safety's sake his reserve was towed at the end of the train.

Paul Bunyan did not dream it, but herein was the stuff of calamity in the crossing of Round River. Snoose was to play a tremendous part in the conquest of the Saginaw. The mighty mineral was even now making ready to show its power.

The serpentine sled blazed on in the dry furrow between two rolling waves.

"The Big Feller can part a river like a bobber parts yer hair," boasted the shanty boys. "Lookit him comb there!"

They boasted too soon.

The Round was the oldest, and therefore the deepest, of all the earth's streams. At noontime Paul Bunyan was perturbed to see the current gurgling near his boot-tops. Water-plowing was harder for him now. He had to kick a little with each stride to send the waves skyhooting. These waves were getting to be bigger bodies of water every minute. Far in the wake of the sled they crashed back together with an ominous roar.

"He's just got a deep streak in himself, this royal old

river has," thought Paul Bunyan optimistically. "I'll be plowing up a solid rise before so long."

The thought murmured from his beard like a great breeze. That was fortunate, for even as he murmured, Paul stepped down a sharp slope in the river bottom, and with such force that he had to crouch and teeter to save himself a fall. But the breeze from his beard helped to blow the waters apart, and he plunged like a barrage into the gap, his boots and legs cleaving the deep water with ferocious strokes.

The waves thundered up and away in such a turmoil that the sun was hidden in a cloud of silver spray. Under the speeding sled the river bottom quaked. The jacks gritted their teeth and held on. Nobody ventured a glance to the rear to see how the snoose-sled was coming on. Paul Bunyan was plunging to reach the solid rise of bottom that was surely just ahead, and all eyes were on the Big Feller.

But for three more hours Paul Bunyan fought a steadily deepening stream. The kingly current rose to his thighs, to his hips, even to his bottom shirt-button, which only the deeps of the ocean had touched heretofore. The great logger's boots drove at the water in vain. He scooped with his hands, and still the river baffled him, seeping through his fingers, foaming over the plowshares and swamping the furrow, until at last the tugs slackened from Babe's yoke.

"The sled is floatin' noo, Ay tank," muttered Hels Helson, his gray eyes two clouds of worry. "And Ay vas vadin' so deep may own self Ay gat vet. Ay bat Ay gat vash some moor. Bay yee, Ay vas sick vit' gattin' vash so mooch in this crazy Saginaw country har!"

It was a long lamentation for Hels Helson, but the Big Feller paid it no attention. He was pessimist Paul Bunyan now and admitted that he would have to swim for it. So he issued brisk orders.

"Clear the decks!" So the brisk order boomed back to the shanty boys. "Clear 'em all, then lash yourselves to the bunks! Got to swim for 'er, men! Lash down, for when the waves roll from my strokes, you're going to get pitched! Stand by! I'm weighing anchor here!"

For another mile Paul Bunyan sturdily fought the river and weighed anchor slowly. He did this by un-shackling the water plows and hanging them from Babe's yoke. At last the serpentine sled was eased up, and floated on heaving swells. Every jack was lashed and ready. The eyes of Babe sparkled. So far this was a joy-ous adventure for the Blue Ox. He treaded water plac-idly, now and again thrusting his muzzle into the stream, lifting it to flip a tongueful of water down the Big Swede's shirt-collar. Hels was too dispirited even to remonstrate with a "Har noo, Babe!" He shuddered miserably and seized Babe's right horn with his left hand at Paul's command. Johnny Inkslinger took the left horn. All were ready to swim.

The river now surged to Paul's shoulders. The tide tugged gigantically at his legs. He submitted grace-fully. Here at last was a river which was more than a match for him. He offered no complaint. The Father of Waters displayed none of the belligerence so common with wild young rivers. It flowed majestically in its great circle, ignoring all other powers, sufficient unto itself. The outlets were mere trickles from the parent stream. Paul Bunyan was sure that Round River would bear his log drives royally, without resistance or even reproach.

So it was with honorable and decent humility that the great logger accepted the necessity of swimming in crossing Round River.

Then, even as he prayerfully started the first stroke, an agonized yell hauled him up. Hels Helson was pointing at the tail of the floating sled, which had curved on with the current, floating into plain view.

"May snoose!" the Big Swede bawled in anguish. "May snoose-sled vas vashed oop noo! No snoose, no logs, bay yee! Ay yust turn all holt loose and drown mayself! Svede feller can't live vit'out snoose! Oh, Ay don' feel so gude noo!"

At once Paul Bunyan realized that he faced a critical situation. Snoose, the unalloyed mineral and most potent of panaceas, was truly the staff of life to Hels Helson, just as the immeasurably weakened artificial snoose of our own time is a necessity to all Scandinavian woodsmen. "No snoose, no logs," is the irrevocable watchword of all such men, so grim is their devotion to the cheek-bulging, hair-sprouting, muscle-springing, blood-curdling derivative of Sweden's mightiest mineral in the era of Pete the First. But the modern artificial product called snoose is no more to be confused with the Bunyan panacea than with the dry and feeble sniffing snuffs of Scotland and France.

Genuine snoose ore was as rare as radium in the day

of Paul Bunyan. The good user wadded the unrefined and unadulterated article into his mouth, retaining the charge between cheek and lower gum. The reaction was specifically sulphuric, but informed botanists require hours to enumerate the various general benefits derived from the absorption of snoose ore. Hels Helson was satisfied simply to praise the panacea as "condition powders." He was the largest individual customer of Pete the First, who owned a monopoly of the snoose mines of Sweden. The King's Irish Navy was not due to ferry over another shipment for months. No one dreamed that veins of the rare ore might be simmering under the bed-rock of Real America.

The Big Swede's summer reserve was on the tail sled. It had been carried away when Paul Bunyan made his first surprised plunge into deep water. There could be no doubt about it now. Paul sighted swarms of flying fish far downstream. Every fish was turning flipflops as he flew. Nothing but a sample of snoose could make a fish perform in such a fashion. Hels Helson's condition powders were dispersed in the Father of Waters. There was nothing for it but to coax Hels into bearing up under his loss like a hero.

But the Big Swede was doing just the opposite. He was carrying out his threat and unloosing his hand from Babe's horn. A drastic act was necessary to save Hels from a rash one. Paul Bunyan saw but one way out.

"Fetch him, Babe," he grimly said.

The Blue Ox obediently clamped his teeth over the collar of the Big Swede, holding the unfortunate's head just above the surface. Paul was heartened by Babe's obvious solicitude for the luckless foreman. He had always believe that the roguish pranks played on Hels by the rugged ox were no more than manifestations of exuberant animal spirits. Now he knew.

"Underneath his spirits Babe has got a heart of gold," affirmed Paul Bunyan.

All true ox-lovers who overheard applauded the humane sentiment.

Now Paul Bunyan made his first stroke. The Blue Ox heaved behind him. Hels Helson, sinking into a coma from the shock of his loss, sagged limply from Babe's uplifted jaws. Johnny Inkslinger, oblivious of all that had occurred, crooked an elbow around the convenient horn and floated unconsciously on, figuring in algebra as he stared at the sun to take observations.

The serpentine sled arched and dipped over ranks of swells. Every shanty rocked. The lashed men were violently pitched, for Paul Bunyan's gentlest swimming stroke sent uproarious and surging waves thundering down his wake.

The sun reddened, sinking to the watery horizon, and Paul Bunyan swam in a sea of fiery hues. Slowly purple shadows quietly clouded the stream. He swam on. The moon rose and bestowed a golden smile on the scene. It got no response. The seasick shanty boys had no stomachs for golden moonlight or for anything else dripping sweets. Babe was still all solicitude for poor Hels. Johnny Inkslinger, weary from working in minus all day, summed up his algebra for an entry in the log. Paul Bunyan plowed on with grim resolution for his goal Night had fallen, and he was yet far out.

For three more nights and two more days the wilderness waited, while the boss logger of the North Woods forged on with tireless strokes. At last, on a shining spring morning of midsummer, the calamitous crossing was ended. When water-parting proceeded again and the desired shore of the Saginaw yielded to Paul Bunyan's tread, there were no expressions of triumph. The bright morning gleamed on a sober and somber camp.

Paul Bunyan shook his shoulders in weariness. He stared gloomily at the unconscious foreman. Babe gently lowered the bedraggled form of Hels on the Saginaw shore. Paul thought to praise the good ox with cheery words, but his own heart was despondent. He was not giving up, however. Without pausing for rest, he wrung the water from his beard and tramped into the primeval forest to look for a camp site.

Paul Bunyan tramped into the shadow of the one mountain of the Saginaw timber country. He did not know it, but this was also the shadow of a war to come. The mountain before him was the creation of Shot Gunderson, iron man of the Saginaw.

Innocent of the shadow's portent, the boss logger of the North Woods tramped sturdily on, his heart kind and brave.

Now he was ready to earn his proudest title, king jack of the Saginaw.

IV

SNOOSE MOUNTAIN

SHOT GUNDERSON was the first man of iron in the North Woods. As prodigious as Paul Bunyan, he boasted, moreover, an invulnerable hide and an irresistible fist. Shot's one weakness was fear, and his one fear was of water. This was entirely natural. Shot Gunderson knew that rust could be his ruin; and, as water is the foremost agent of rust, Shot shunned showers as a saint shuns sin.

The fact is boldly presented, not as a curiosity, but as solemn matter of history. It became a portentous matter upon Paul Bunyan's entry into the Saginaw. For the mountainous landmark by which the boss logger had steered in his epochal swim was an artificial creation; it was the dump of a mine Shot Gunderson had worked for a host of seasons in a fruitless digging for edible iron ore.

Instead, Shot had unearthed a kind of ore which had a powerfully enjoyable flavor, but generally failed to condition him. He could not live without iron. The new mineral slowly let his blood turn to water and corroded his pipes inside. The stuff was plainly unsuited to men of iron. So Shot had abandoned the mine, crossed the northern arch of Round River when it was solidly frozen, discovered a range of iron mountains, and proceeded to tone his system up.

Paul Bunyan was to learn all this later with consternation. Tramping now in the shadow of the towering mine dump, he saw only the shadow of an untimbered but honest mountain. He had, as a matter of fact, heard rumors about the iron man of the Saginaw, but he expected no trouble from Shot Gunderson. In the stump speech delivered to his jacks on the eve of quitting Quebec he had touched on the subject with characteristic optimism.

"Even if we meet," the Big Feller had declared from the stump, "Shot and me can keep the peace. I'll be in the Saginaw to get out the logs. Shot'll be there to get out the iron. I chop trees. He shovels ore. Where's the trouble there? Let him have his iron, let me have my logs, and let us all have peace, by the old Proverbs!"

But Paul Bunyan was roaring peace when there was no peace. In the hard rough region of the north Shot Gunderson had uncovered enough iron ore to make himself into a battleship of a man. At last he was rusting from lack of action. All he needed to brighten him up was the news that another hero had invaded the Saginaw. Then he would get up steam and go looking for the exercise he craved.

The boss logger was in no immediate danger, however. The iron man would have to get the news first. Then he would have to wait for a winter freeze hard enough to make ice in Round River that would hold him up. Shot Gunderson could swim no more than an anvil. Never would he risk his weight on ice less than seventeen feet thick. One simple wetting would rust his joints. Complete immersion would utterly corrode him.

Winter was months away, and the season was likely to be mild when it came. The weather was obviously set for a kind year. For the present the prospective king jack of the Saginaw was entirely safe.

But rumors were already speeding northward. Even now the first whales to use Round River for calving- and nursing-grounds were leaping and blowing in the upper curve of the Father of Waters. Shot Gunderson saw them there.

"Somebody's been a monkeyin' with the Big Auger," rasped the man of iron. "Whales could of never got up here if somebody had never monkeyed with that there river." A sinister scowl shadowed his cannon-ball eyes. "And if that somebody comes over to do tricks in the Saginaw," Shot Gunderson rasped on, "I'll iron the monkey wrinkles outer him, by the old anvil prong!"

But Round River was flowing through midsummer in spring flood. Shot Gunderson had to bide his time.

Paul Bunyan could not imagine more trouble cloud-ing up. He was already oppressed by as much as he could bear. Without a foreman he could not get out the logs. And this was his one inflexibly powerful purpose in life. To get out the logs he had fought the Big Auger down. To get out the logs he had made a famous cross-ing of Round River. Without his prime purpose Paul

Bunyan would have left the one river untwisted and the other uncrossed forever. Exploration, adventure, and conquest were nothing in themselves to him. His entry of the Saginaw was futile unless he logged the land.

As the spring sunlight robed the summer day in full splendor, Paul Bunyan rounded the mountain. A shimmering amber lake shone into his eyes with such uplifting beauty that his spirit instinctively responded. Along its bordering slopes groves of butternuts, oaks, elms, maples, and birch reached afar, their lighter greens merging with a black mass of timber which the logger at once recognized as prime onion pine. Here indeed was a superb site for a camp. The only lack was an outlet to Round River.

Paul did not know that the lake was really the flooded mine working of Shot Gunderson. Nor did he at first note the peculiarities of the mountain as he turned to survey it. Then a morning breeze began to rustle by. It wafted a familiar odor from somewhere. Paul Bunyan's nose stung as it used to sting when—

"When was it now?" he thought quizzically. "When did I whiff the like of that before?"

Suddenly his frown of perplexity deepened. The dawn breeze blowing down from the woods had grown into a sunrise wind. It turned, rolling from the woods and the lake. Paul Bunyan's nose was stung no more. Instead, it was caressed and exhilarated by the mingled perfumes of pines, flowers, grass, and fresh water. Sniffing and sighing with pleasure, the logger observed that the wind was now blowing the steam from the mountain slopes away from him. Instantly he understood.

The familiar smell belonged to the mountain there!

At once Paul Bunyan's sagacity caught fire. It recognized and classified the familiar smell. It made him roar into action.

"Snoose Mountain!" roared Paul Bunyan. "That's what I've discovered, by the manna of the wilderness and the milk of the old Promised Land!" Now he trumpeted through his hands. "Yay, Babe! Fetch me Hels here!"

An eager moo answered the call. Paul started back around the mountain to meet Babe and Hels. He was all optimism again, his jubilation over the miraculous discovery admitting no doubts whatever. A mountain of snoose in the Saginaw not only meant the early recovery of the Big Swede, but meant Liberty also. So far Pete the First had demanded an enormous tax for every snoose shipment ferried over from Sweden by the Royal Navy. Snoose Mountain promised freedom and independence without a reservation to the great logger and his jacks.

"Certainly a time to remember, this here day is," Paul reflected, hustling on. "Got to rig up a regular date for it. Can't remember the big day of Liberty just by a season. Got to have a figure for it, by the generology of the old Methusly!"

Even now Johnny Inkslinger was working algebra to learn just where in time this famous day was. The figuring was tough. As time had not yet acquired numerical chronology, Johnny, his head roaring with algebra, called these the plus years of the minus era. Then he let

x, y, and z stand for the three unknown quantities of the year, the month, and the date of the big day. Johnny was cudgeling his brain for a known quantity to start his algebra on when Paul Bunyan's commanding shout rolled around the mountain.

Johnny Inkslinger never did get his equations unsnarled. Paul and his jacks finally called the big day of Liberty the Fourther July, and let it go at that.

In the shadow of the mountain Paul Bunyan impatiently waited. It seemed hours before Babe's sky-blue bulk loomed over the hardwoods of the river bottom. The ox came sidewise, his neck bowed to the left, Hels Helson dragging limply from his jaws. Great tears fell from Babe's eyes, and in such quantities that they gathered and roared in a foaming torrent under the serpentine sled. The shanty boys had been unlashing themselves, hoping to start the ceremony of leg-stretching soon. Now they took to their bunks again, imagining that the Big Feller was parting another river.

Paul heard the groans of the jacks, but he had more pressing business at hand. This was to revive Hels Helson. Johnny Inkslinger swung round with his first-aid kit.

"All you need, Johnny, is to give him snoose," ventured Paul Bunyan. "Can't you let first aid go this here trip?"

Johnny Inkslinger looked offended. Doctoring was his great duty, next to figuring, and he resented any meddling with its established ceremonies and forms. With a weary sigh, Paul Bunyan stepped back, too kind to hurt Johnny's feelings. The ceremony began.

First the timekeeper laid Hels Helson on a flat surface, face downward, his head slightly downhill. He then turned Hels's head to one side to protect his nose and mouth from dirt. Johnny's next move was to kneel formally, straddling the Big Swede's back, and facing the unfortunate's head. Murmuring incantations, the doctor now placed his hands over the lower ribs of Hels, one on each side of the backbone, leaving a space of some nineteen feet between the hands. Muttering a rhythmic chant, Dr. Johnny projected the weight of his body slightly downward and forward, without sliding, holding his arms stiff and straight, his eyes gleaming mysteriously through his spectacles. Then, with a portentous grimace, he snapped his hands free. The ribs of Hels Helson instantly responded, expanding eleven spheric yards, sucking in air with a cyclonic blast. Deflation followed with a sigh of such mournful tone that Babe's tears poured afresh. The Blue Ox was perilously nigh a mood of desperation.

Dr. Johnny proceeded with his ceremonies. With every stiff-armed pressure forward he solemnly uttered this incantation:

"Out goes the bad air!"

Releasing and reversing, his voice rose on a triumphant note:

"In goes the good!"

As the ceremony continued, Johnny Inkslinger became rapt in a mystical glow. He stared skyward, his gaze suffused with a sublime light. Now his incantations were entirely cabalistic.

"The full capacity of his lungs is three hundred and twenty cubic yards!" chanted Dr. Johnny. "There are more than five hundred separate muscles in his body, with an equal number of nerves and blood-vessels! Each perspiratory duct is a quarter yard in length, and all together run nigh to nine hundred and ninety miles! Out goes the bad air! In goes the good!"

"Flummery and folderol," grumbled Paul Bunyan. "Why don't he give Hels snoose and be done with it?"

Yet he rigorously respected the private rights and privileges claimed by Johnny Inkslinger, and he would not interfere.

It was different with Babe, however. Naturally the Blue Ox did not possess a mind of sufficient grandeur and power to comprehend the sublime ceremonies venerated by mankind. Babe had little respect for the intricate intellectual rituals of Johnny Inkslinger and no patience with them whatever.

Goaded by the torment of waiting, Babe acted to force matters. Yet his cunning did not desert him. He sidled his rear toward Snoose Mountain and slyly began to brush its slope down with unobtrusive digs and shoves from his tail. Johnny was still chanting at the sky. Paul, his brooding gaze fixed on the mountain's peak, had fallen into a brown study. Nobody noticed the hill of snoose ore rising swiftly alongside Hels Helson's gaping mouth. Neither Johnny nor Paul suspected what was up until a jawful of snoose was down. Then Babe furtively lowered his muzzle and pushed the whole hill into the mouth of the Big Swede.

Instantly three cataclysms shook the valley from

rim to rim, from thin air to bedrock.

The first cataclysm was inaugurated by Hels Helson. As the fire and brimstone of the explosive panacea surged into his veins his whole being responded with a hilarious heave of delight. So tremendous was the heave that Johnny Inkslinger was catapulted over the mountain top and into the lake. He was still in a mystical daze.

"Out goes the bad air!" he was chanting as Hels heaved him.

"In goes the good!" he was singing as he struck.

Then ensued a parting of the waters which would have done credit to Paul himself. The whole lake surged two ways. Running around the mountain, Paul Bunyan charged over the emptied lake bed and seized the thunderstruck timekeeper before the waves could foam back in a raging flood and close over him. Paul braced himself, and the muddy waters tore at his boots in vain. Now the waves roared on into Snoose Mountain. The right slope crumbled. The waters, backed up for many seasons, heaved on, eating a channel around the mountain for an escape to Round River. An avalanche crashed down. Yet the new river roared on.

"The mountain'll wash away," said Paul Bunyan fearfully. "There goes Liberty no sooner than she's found! Got to think fast!"

The third cataclysm intervened. This one had its source in Babe the Blue Ox and was, in consequence, the most tremendous of all. For the first time in his innocent life Babe had sampled the flavors of snoose. Heretofore its potent stimulation had always been denied him. Paul

Bunyan could easily surmise the dire effect of any such indulgence. When snoose exhilarated such a stolid man as Hels Helson, it would be certain to sweep such a naturally exuberant and mercurial creature as Babe into a perilous ecstasy.

The shrewd surmise was correct. Babe proved it now. A mere hundredweight of snooose had worked into his mouth as he ministered to Hels Helson. Flashing red circles began to whirl before his eyes. They pleased Babe and, his wits rapidly addling, he lowered his jaws to the mountain slope and his teeth gnawed in like so many steam-shovel dippers. Then the Blue Ox swallowed, and the damage was done.

Even Hels Helson dared not swallow snoose. Shot Gunderson could do it, but he was so constituted that only iron would cause any powerful reaction in his system. Babe was no iron ox, but one of sensitive flesh, blood, and nerves. By the time his four stomachs were pregnant with the violent mineral, his last shred of self-control sizzled away. Babe was all sensation now.

For one thing, he had the certain feeling that the snoose had set his hair on fire. This sensation swiftly changed to one which made him believe that icicles were popping from all his pores. Babe's knees knocked thunderously. Yet the snoose in him had only begun to ferment and work. It was a full minute before the snoose fumes seeped to his hoofs and horns. The Blue Ox felt himself blazing again. He seemed to be both plumed and shod with fire. Then Babe started a blind charge for Round River to put himself out.

The serpentine sled bounded as the earth quaked in

great waves. The bunks rocked and tottered from wall to wall.

"She's a shipwreck!" bellowed the hard-used shanty boys.

Grimly holding on as the shanties pitched and tossed, they began to rip up their bunks and tie them into rafts.

Paul Bunyan shrewdly draped Johnny Inkslinger alongside the mountain so that he lay like a bulwark against the new river, and galloped after the sled.

"Got to save the Blue Ox from himself," roared Paul as he charged on. "Got to save him from the river there!"

In the meantime the Big Swede was already up and doing, his eyes glittering like ax-blades as new life coursed through his veins. His cheek was primed again. It bulged like an oak stump as Hels unloosed a blast against the wind.

"Bay yee, Ay feel so gude noo!" chuckled Hels Helson.

Then he heard Paul Bunyan. Ahead of the logger a huge blue cloud seemed to be bounding among the green of the trees. Then a blue tornado appeared to twist out of the sky. Ten acres of oaks crashed down.

"Babe, you bat you!" roared Hels. "No tornado could do this har! Yust Babe can knock down ten acre trees vit' his tail, yesiree!"

Now Hels Helson also charged to save Babe from himself. So revitalized was the foreman that he caught up with Paul in two running jumps, and in two more had passed him.

"Ay yump, and Ay yump, and *yeeminee!*" he bellowed gayly as he passed Paul Bunyan in a bound.

Paul marveled to hear Hels Helson, and he also hoped as the inspired foreman jumped on. Ahead of him Babe was plunging on for Round River with such speed that he was like nothing so much as a blue comet come to earth. Certainly no human power could stop him, but Hels was superhuman now. After his loss and deprivation this charge of snoose stimulated him as no other had ever done. Besides, it was the snoose of the old Saginaw. Truly this was Hels Helson's hour.

On the very brink of the river the Big Swede's last running jump was broken in mid air as his powerful hands clutched the horns of the Blue Ox. An irresistible twist of his wrists brought Babe down. Babe's tail threshed wildly and his hoofs pawed convulsively at the empty air, but every struggle only gave Hels Helson a solider grip on his horns. There was nothing for Paul Bunyan to do but to take in the situation.

The great logger did that instantly.

"You've got to bulldog him down till the effect wears off," he said. "Think you can hold him, Hels?"

The Big Swede responded with a solid grin.

"You bat you!" he said proudly. "Give Svede feller like me plenty snoose and he hold anyt'ing, yesiree!"

Hels had made no empty boast. For five weeks he kept his grip on the horns of the Blue Ox and held him down. Whenever Hels weakened, Paul Bunyan simply primed him with fresh snoose. Day by day Babe's convulsions slackened, and at last he lay limp and relaxed, mooing feebly for baled hay. Hels got up proudly and stretched himself.

"Noo, bay yee, Ay vas ready to log," he said ardently. "Plenty snoose, plenty log, yesiree!"

Paul Bunyan smiled fondly through his beard. He had a rich reward prepared for Hels Helson. The boss logger said nothing about it until he had led the foreman to the new camp. Then Hels let out a roar of wrath as he saw that Snoose Mountain was no more. In its place towered the peak that was to have great fame in history as the Old Saginaw Sawdust Pile.

"Just a second there, Hels," smiled Paul Bunyan. "Wait'll I give you a look at the new snoose-sled."

Hels Helson's jaws sagged as he gaped at a shining new sled packed from stem to stern with hogsheads.

"Seventeen and a half thousand of 'em," said Paul Bunyan, with pride. "But this is just a sled-load. Take a look next at your own private and personal snoose arsenal, Hels."

The boss logger led the way to the high and dry side of the Sawdust Pile. From its slope bulked the log walls of an arsenal which even surpassed the grand one belonging to King Pete's Royal Irish Navy. Inside snoose barrels were stacked in innumerable tiers and illimitable rows.

"The sawdust'll keep the snoose fresh," said Paul Bunyan. "It was just a little idea of mine to save the mountain from water and weather," he went on modestly. "I found some old iron shovels, so I rigged up a barrel-mill, set the jacks to chopping ash, and there's the snoose and a new mountain, and here we are, Hels. What do you say?"

"Ay say ve gat out the logs noo," responded the Big

Swede earnestly. "Ay feel so gude."

The two mighty loggers shook hands.

"It shore looks like a mighty happy endin' to that tremenjus Fourther July," the shanty boys said.

All seemed fine and well in the old Saginaw. No one suspected that north of Round River Shot Gunderson was still watching whales, munching raw iron, and scowling darkly at the notion of somebody monkeying with his private property down there.

V

THE TROTTING TREES

LOGGING went on. The first famous job in the Saginaw
was on the Big Onion, the new river floating by the Old
Sawdust Pile. The history of the harvest of the tear-
squeezing pines that grew in the fork of the Big Onion
and the Little Garlic is a twice-told tale, so it may not
be repeated here. It is enough to say that the last onion
pine in the Saginaw was triumphantly trundled to the
skidways, and then Paul Bunyan went on a cruising ex-
pedition to the north.

He discovered a grand scene for next year's logging
in the fork of the Big Sunny and the Little Moon. Then
Paul turned his footsteps homeward. Autumn had succeeded the elongated spring, and frost was snapping in
the air. Snow might be falling any day. Then it would
be time to move the mountains of onion pines from the
skidways to the banking-grounds on the big river.

In the meantime a tremendous event was taking place
in the leaderless logging camp. A perplexing and perilous species of pine invaded overnight the stump lands
in the big bend where the Little Garlic poured into the

main stream. These pines were of a nature to baffle any botanist who was not also a boss logger.

They were trotting trees. These conifers formed a unique species, one as localized as the Big Trees of California. Some special quality—a subsoil of snoose, perhaps—in the land of the trotting trees deprived them of the turgescence natural to normal pines; instead of the usual tension and rigidity of cells and tenacity of roots, their trunks and boughs pulsed and glowed with *élan vital;* and the four jointed roots peculiar to the individual pine spurned the earth even as they fed on its soil.

So the trees trotted. They never found a passage through the dense standing timber surrounding their bit of country, however, until the valley of the Big Onion was logged off. Then the trotting trees moved in overnight.

Ever since that memorable night loggers have referred to regular trees as "standing timber," to distinguish the stationary varieties from the running timber of the old Saginaw.

Hels Helson was the first to discover the invasion. He rose at dawn to brush Babe down. This was the morning for the Big Feller's return. Maybe he would have found tough logging for next year, and the sight of Babe shining like a rain-washed sky would cheer him up. Thinking that, the loyal Big Swede primed himself with three scoops of snoose and started in a prancing stride for the stable.

Instantly Hels halted, his right foot poised in mid

air. A half-dozen pines were swaying on the toe of his boot as though they had grown there. Hels Helson owned a literal mind. That trees might hop, skip, and jump never occurred to him. He could not believe his eyes as he saw these pines looming from his boot-toe; and he still doubted as the trees set out at a trot up his inclined leg. On up his bootlaces they ambled until the edge of his wool sock was achieved. Then Hels hastily set his foot down. The pines were shaken inside his sock.

At once his leg began to tickle. In size the trees resembled the dwarf jack pines of our own time, and they were also thorny. The thorns tickled Hels Helson's leg tremendously. He clawed frantically at the boot, but the pines were only forced down to the bottom of his foot. A tickling shin Hels could bear, but a tickling foot bottom he could not abide. In another second he was rolling and laughing convulsively through the running timber.

The effect resembled that of a man of regular size rolling through a swarm of black biting ants. To escape being shivered into splinters the trotting trees leaped on Hels as he rolled. Their instinct made them trot into all the crevices of his clothes and to swarm all over him, pricking him everywhere with their thorns as he kicked, pawed, and bellowed. The Big Swede's convulsive bawls rose in shaking blasts, and the earth trembled as his fists and heels flailed it. In the shanties the jacks began to yell.

"Babe's got the foreman down and is chawin' him!" they surmised, at the tops of their lungs. "She's another snoose fight there!"

The loud surmise was wrong. After his harrowing experience Babe was indeed sensitive to the point of being old womanish concerning snoose. But the Blue Ox was having other troubles now. While yet in his night's slumber, a band of the invading pines had trotted up on his back and rooted themselves in what seemed to be fine hollows for trees. They were still clinging there when Babe reared up at Hels's first bellow. Babe itched feverishly.

He squirmed his hind quarters toward his muzzle, which was wrinkled until every tooth was bared. Then he laid back his ears and began to gnaw viciously at the tormenting trees, but they were hard to find among his great matted hairs. It was many seasons, indeed, before Babe was rid of the last of his trees. Whenever Paul Bunyan would see the Blue Ox gnawing at his back like that or twisting his head to one side, shutting his eyes, and scratching violently at his neck with a hind foot, then Paul would murmur:

"He ain't rid of his trees yet, the poor feller. No, sir, Babe has still got trees, and it's just up to me to give him another dose of tree powder."

But now it was Hels Helson who had them the worst. His groans and yells were nigh to upsetting the camp.

"Oh, bay yee!" yelled Hels Helson. "Ay eder gat tickle' to deat' oor Ay gat eat oop alive, Ay bat you, noo!"

It looked like tickling to death as the trees reached his ribs.

"If he laughs much louder, he'll split 'em," declared the shanty boys ominously. "Them sides of his'n, we mean. Already he sounds like splittin' rails."

The jacks were all out in their underclothes. The shaggy red woolens harmonized superbly with the fiery hues of the autumn sunrise. But nobody had an eye for the beauty of the scene in the shanty yard. Even the uproarious spectacle of the Big Swede was forgotten as the eyes of the shanty boys bulged at the strangest stampede ever known to history.

Naturally the trotting trees were wild creatures of instinct. They could no more comprehend Hels Helson than ants could comprehend men. It was simply the primordial impulse to expand the species that had moved them blindly into a land where nothing was left but the barren stumps of onion pines. Their violent reception from the Big Swede had stampeded the whole herd of wild roving pines. They rampaged blindly now, moving in a torrential mass around the camp. Like all wild creatures on stampede, they moved in a circle, and this instinct saved the trees from a smash-up over the river bank.

For minutes the shanty boys stared as incredulously as Hels Helson had stared. Not one burly, red-sheathed form among the men quivered as all gaped, their chins sagging to their chests in profound amazement, their eyes bulging until they could have been sliced like sausage ends. Against the frosty blue of the brightening sky the piny crowns were waving and plunging plumes. Clouds of cones, needles, and twigs leaped up like bursting cannon-balls, and the splintering crashes of boughs broken in collisions equaled the uproar of a cannon-

ade as the trotting trees stampeded on. Under the swaying and jerking trunks the roots worked in powerful
frenzies, the front ones lifting until the center joints
would almost touch the trunks, then driving down like
pistons, the knotty feet of the roots pounding the earth
with the solidity of mallet blows. The dust flew, rolling
up country in a spreading cloud.

Now from out of that cloud a sneeze hurtled with
reverberations that could be shaken forth by only one
nose on earth.

"There's the Big Feller," breathed the shanty boys,
coming to life. "Nobody else has got sech a shaker of
a sneeze as that there one."

At once the jacks began to use their heads. Since coming to the Saginaw, men had been trying to learn to
think. Paul Bunyan considered it a perilous occupation
for his jacks, but they now proved that their heads were
mighty usable in an emergency.

"Leave these here trottin' trees to the Big Feller,"
they agreed, thinking as one man. "Let's don't let on
we know a thing about 'em. He's the only party to figure
'em out."

So the jacks hustled back to their bunks and pretended to snore as Paul Bunyan emerged from the dust
cloud. Just once he paused for another incomparable
sneeze, and then he unloosed his sagacity on the situation.

Instant action was demanded, and Paul Bunyan had
hardly pocketed his bandanna before it started. The
jacks had pretended only three snores before orders

were roaring through the shanties. The jacks hearkened.

"Roll out or roll up for a new kind of loggin', men! Breakfast on the fly! You head choppers there! Off with the blades from your grass rope ax-handles! Rig up the ropes with lasso loops! We got a job here where we must catch our trees before we can chop 'em. And catch 'em we will, by the scorched paw of the sun-stopping old Joshuay! What do you say there?"

"Ketch 'em, you betcher!" the jacks roared back.

They winked shrewdly at one another and declared they had thought things out just right. The Big Feller was taking all responsibility. The men never thought of anything else.

While all grabbed breakfast on the fly, and the boss choppers transformed their grass rope ax-handles into lassos, Paul Bunyan was toting Hels to Round River to wash the trees off him. Hels was still being terribly tickled, but the prospect of a washing was enough to hush his laughter. Now he only groaned.

"Ay don' feel so gude," groaned the Big Swede. "Bay yee, may life in Saginaw har is yust vun vash after an-udder vash, yesiree."

But he submitted while Paul Bunyan ridded him of trees. Every pine pawed viciously with its four roots as the current washed it away, but its struggles soon ended. The trotting trees had no instinct whatever for swimming. The quiet dark mass that floated off Hels Helson's ribs might easily have been mistaken for common onion pines.

Upon returning to camp the great logger and his foreman found the men waiting. The stampede roared on with increasing violence, the trees trotting at a more tremendous rate every minute. Boss choppers and ax-men were arrayed for action. Every jack was in his mackinaw, calked boots, stagged pants, and tasseled cap. As the last gang marched from the cookhouse, the crew paraded in full formation. Paul Bunyan smiled as he saw that each shanty boy had his lunch around his neck as usual.

In the chopping season every axman was presented with a huge flapjack upon rising from breakfast, a cake with a hole in the center like a doughnut's. Ready for labor, the bully jack would thrust his head through the hole, settle the stiff cake about his neck like a ruff, and then fall to with his ax. At lunch-time he continued to chop, heaving the flapjack up and around with his shoulders and munching mouthfuls between blows. So every axman lunched without missing a lick. No indus-trialist of our own time has equaled Paul Bunyan in devising methods to save the golden minutes.

But this morning the method was out of place. The choppers needed neck room for the special job, so the boss logger ordered his men to fold the flapjacks and then twist one end of each cake into a hook. This done, the men engaged the hooks over their sashes so that the flapjacks covered their right hip pockets. With this simple device the jacks would get sustenance without knowing it. They were forever reaching into their hip pockets for chaws. Now, instead of chaws, they would grab fistfuls of flapjack.

Sagacious Paul Bunyan having disposed of the lunch problem in jig time, he now gave a brief stump speech of instruction and inspiration. The boss choppers never missed a word. Every one was primed as he coiled his grass rope ax-handle and bawled for his gang to get busy there.

The boss choppers were the great leaders in labor among the regular men of the camp. At the head of the leaders, in turn, were seven king choppers, who were famously known as the Seven Axmen. When chopping, the great seven maintained a steady march, each one gripping his limber rope ax-handle in both fists and whirling the blade with such force that it flashed like the teeth of a circular saw. These prodigious little men— not a one measured over three feet between instep and kneecap—simply mowed down the pines as they marched. In the wake of each king chopper his gang would fell the smaller trees and limb and buck all of them. With such axmen, and with such a skidder as Babe the Blue Ox, Paul Bunyan could log more in a season than a modern boss logger can in a century.

Certainly any modern boss logger would have been baffled by the stampede of trotting trees. But not so the first and greatest of the tribe. His sagacity was approaching its prime. Wherever there were trees, he would get out the logs. Trotters, pacers, or gallopers, they could not baffle Paul Bunyan.

Now his king choppers neared the line of stampede. Every bully halted, crouched low, and peered shrewdly at the plunging and pounding roots of the runaway pines. It was not an ax-blade he whirled from the end of his grass rope handle this trip. In the blade's place was a lasso loop. Over his head each boss chopper twirled a loop with his right hand, while the long coils of the grass rope dangled from his left. Every gang formed on the flanks of the boss chopper to which it belonged, axmen to the right, canthook men to the left. All was ready.

"Timb-er-r-r!" roared Paul Bunyan. "Let 'er go!"

A medley of hissing whines pierced the thunder of the stampede. The sounds whistled up as the boss choppers made their casts at the running roots of picked pines. Every noose fell true. Paul Bunyan sighed with pride. His ax-twirlers could not fail. As lassoers they were also paragons. All around the circle of the stampede the boss choppers were digging their calks into the earth, bracing themselves, leaning back, solidly gripping the taut and quivering ax-handles, while the noosed roots of prone pines kicked and pawed in vain for freedom.

"Hold 'em there!" commanded the boss logger. "Canthook men to the head and foot! Axmen, get out the logs!"

The jacks responded as nobly as their leaders. The canthook crews charged. They swung their tools and drove the prongs into the bark of the prone pines. Then they bore down on the handles. With the head choppers tightening their nooses on the wild roots, and with the canthook men solidly holding the trunks, the axmen plunged bravely in, lopping off limbs and whacking the trees into logs with their lustiest swings. The bosses flipped their ropes from the now limp roots and made ready for a second cast.

"Let 'er go again!" ordered Paul Bunyan.

Logging went on. For a week the boss logger and his jacks fought the trotting trees to a standstill. Then the stampede was broken, and the worst was over. The shanty boys had suffered few casualties. Here and there a cast had missed and a boss chopper had been knocked down and run over. Now and then some raging brute of a lassoed tree would kick a root free and wreak havoc among the canthookers and axmen. But the pick of Europe's wildest men could not be intimidated by such trifles as root kicks and tree bites. The jacks regarded all such bungs and bruises as red badges of courage and purple decorations of honor. Whenever one was knocked and pitched on his ear, he would reach nonchalantly for a chaw and come up with a fistful of flapjack. Cramming that into his cheek, he would seize his tool and plunge savagely back into action.

At last only young saplings and sprigs were left from the once great grove. Paul Bunyan let the young trotting trees go. Some of the sentimental men took seedlings into the shanties and tried to conjure them into being pets, but they proved to be worse than porcupines and polecats to have round. Somebody was forever stepping on one of the pets with his bare feet, or else sitting on one of the thorny creatures, until the shanty nights were given over almost entirely to sticker-plucking. Besides, the larger loose trees still tormented Hels Helson like ants, and the Blue Ox like fleas. Paul Bunyan at last ordered all the pets and camp-followers to be herded back to their original timberland.

Stray descendants of the trotting trees survive to this day. They are incredibly deceitful, wild, and shy. One can imitate a jack pine so perfectly that the shrewdest woodsman may not detect it. On the darkest night a trotting tree may sometimes be caught on the move, but it will either vanish like a shadow or take root instantly when approached.

"A trottin' tree is here today and gone tomorrer," shrewd woodsmen have declared since the time of Paul Bunyan. "When you see a pine in a partickler place yistiddy and you can't find it tomorrer, don't think yer goin' bats and buggy. It was jest a trottin' tree you saw, and off it ambled sometimer th' night."

They no longer trot, however. The modern moving pines are called trotting trees merely as a matter of courtesy. These trees creep.

VI

THE HUNTING OF THE MINCE

WINTER rapidly drew nigh, but the snows refused to fall early. There was an interim of idleness in the camp on the Big Onion. The jacks had done all their breeches-patching, calk-sharpening, peavey-polishing, and whisker-trimming in preparation for the skidding season. Then they sort of languished and began to remember that in the first place they had been men. Human notions buzzed and hummed perilously in their skulls. Paul Bunyan was troubled.

"She's no good logging," he sighed each morning as the sun would glitter up in a clear sky. "I got to rig up something else that's good for this here interim. Yes, sir, I simply must stop the jacks from having notions."

Another difficulty which bothered Paul these late autumn days was a distinct coldness which persisted between Babe and Hels. The Blue Ox still suffered from nightmares about his terrific summer's experience with snoose. Often he would awaken with shudders which shook the entire camp; then for an hour he would stand with his tail between his legs, back hair bristling, ears flattened, his muzzle lifting in mournful moos at the moon. Only Paul Bunyan could soothe Babe back to sleep at such times. At work in the woods the nervous ox would frequently let fly with both hind hoofs at Hels Helson's hip pockets, where the foreman kept hogsheads of snoose for casual refreshment. Babe's aim was apt and pat. Nearly every kick would send a hip pocket flying. Hels spent hours searching for lost hip pockets in the woods.

"Bay yee, Ay vas gat mad yat, Ay bat you noo," he complained at last.

Paul Bunyan was sympathetic. He knew that hip pockets, next to calked boots, were a woodsman's most sacred possession, serving him as tool-box, treasure-chest, and cupboard.

"Guess I'll have to take Babe off on a trip so's he'll have a chance to forgive and forget," reflected Paul. "Take his mind off snoose for once. Give him something new. Yes, sir, I'll invent a new kind of trip for Babe's special benefit. That ought to please him up, by the ruddy old apple of Adam!"

His sagacity being already whetted from solving the hard problem of trotting trees, Paul Bunyan was no more than a day and night inventing the hunting trip as the greatest institution in the North Woods both for interims of idleness and for chances to forgive and forget. To this day men go hunting in the North Woods when they are idle, and to shed worries as the Blue Ox did his snoose troubles. Nothing is better for all that than good hunting.

On a morning of snapping frost the boss logger was ready. A home-made but sure-fire scatter cannon with thirty barrels rode his right shoulder. The Blue Ox frisked and scampered at his heels. The jacks were already gabbing like mad as they argued over the prospects of the Big Feller bagging a bunch of minces for a mighty meal of thanksgiving.

He had made them a stump speech about that at dawn. It was time to show some thanks, the Big Feller said, for the fine start they had made in the Old Saginaw. And how could men show thanks better than by sitting down and enjoying a hearty meal for themselves? The shanty boys cheered in roars. Paul Bunyan smiled behind his beard, thinking how he knew men inside as well as out. Then he wound up his stump speech by promising a great mince dinner for the thanksgiving meal, provided that he found good hunting. It looked mighty likely. North of Big Sunny Valley was a lake land where the swigging mince reigned supreme. Paul had heard the gurgling mullows of the fat brown game everywhere there, he declared. Beyond a doubt he could bag a plenty with his thirty-barreled scatter cannon.

By the time the Big Feller was through, the jacks were watering so at the mouth that they simply sprayed out the cheers. Paul shouldered his hunting piece and game-bag.

"To heel, Babe," he said. "To heel there. And we never look back till we have enough mince meat for every man in camp to wrap his lips around!"

It was the one unthinking boast ever made by Paul Bunyan. The hunting spirit already possessed him.

The swigging mince, who sloshed as he ambled and whose voice was a juicy mullow, was at the same time the most proud and sensitive creature in the North Woods. Like the swamp sauger and the hodag of the hills, the mince was a survivor of the prehistoric period in the Saginaw. Botanists maintain that the mince was the ancestor of both the beaver and the bear. If so, he lived to see this progeny of his flourish superbly in the North Woods. But the mince did not wander. He kept to his homeland, which circled the waters of Cider Lake, north of Big Sunny Valley.

Paul Bunyan had given this land little attention during his cruise. Its timber, as a logger saw it, was mainly bush and scrub. Berry brambles entwined the gnarled trunks of wild apple and plum trees, and spicy springs burbled from the odorous earth. The biggest streams were no more than brooklets. They smelled fine and tasted well, but they owned no advantages for log driving. Had Paul not invented hunting, he would have passed the homeland of the mince by, leaving it unknown to history.

Even so, only glimpses of the rich life there are remembered.

The swigging mince was king. Like the sauger and the beaver, he owned great fighting power in his tail. The mince had a huge crescent of a mouth which served splendidly for catching apples, plums and berries as they fell, but his teeth were no good for anything tougher than fruit. The mince's feet were also serviceable for scooping in the loose, fruity earth, but they had no claws for ripping, tearing and slashing. He was, in fact, pan-footed, pot-legged, kettle-necked, barrel-bellied, tub-haunched, so entirely underslung and roly-poly that he could never have survived had it not been for his tail.

In that article the mince had a prime possession. The tail was not unlike a beaver's, so far as the tip was concerned; but this prodigious paddle or plate or dipper or wad—the tip was so supple it was now like one thing, now like another, as the need arose—was connected to the mince's rump by a handle, so to speak, which was as limber as green willow and as tough as old hickory.

With that tail of his the mince habitually supped and preened himself on the lake shore at eventide. In the sunset glow the shore of Cider Lake was always adorned by a circle of minces sitting serenely on their haunches, while they solemnly dipped their tails into the odorous brown waters, idly flipped them upward, opened their maws toward the darkling sky, caught the flipped sups, and swigged them down. When they were well soaked, the minces would shower their rich coats of curly brown with the lake waters, the while they gurgled mullows of sweet content at the rising moon. So they supped and cooled themselves on the hottest summer nights, and were always juicy and fat in the driest autumns. As they gurgled into sleep, the eyes of the minces would close like big bubbles blowing out in a breeze.

But their tails ever remained on guard, swaying over the sleeping bulks of their owners like ponderous leaf fans. No beast of prey could approach without the tails taking alarm, sounding the tocsin, and savagely repulsing the prowler all in an instant. In battle a mince's tail would double back, the powerful tip wadding up first, then heaving in a dripping toss for the enemy's face. Thoroughly soused, splashed, blinded, and choked, the enemy was helpless, while the aroused mince turned his tail into a paddle and thoroughly swinged and belammed the presumptuous intruder. The battle mullow of a mince was proud and loud, and all other creatures of the lake lands learned to fear it.

In time all these creatures learned a vast respect and veneration for tails and strove to develop good ones for themselves. Some of them succeeded. The roaring rabbit of the North Woods was, for example, no such timorous, cowering, and cringing beast as the rabbit of our own time. That rabbit had a great tail for himself. He preyed on panthers. The rabbit would lurk for one, and when the prey appeared, he would twist his long ropy tail about the beast's neck, jerk him down, and then kick the life out of the noosed panther with smashing hind-foot drives. Panthers trembled and their blood curdled when the rabbit of Paul Bunyan's time roared down the forest aisles at night.

The deer that so thickly populated those woods also had fine tails for themselves. Their tails were for beauty, as deer browsed for their meals. Each buck and doe had a tail like a plume, and these plumy tails were the bright spots of beauty in the forest. The bears had huge, stiff, bushy tails which were highly useful. There were never creatures cleaner than the bears of that time, because they were constantly using their tails for the cleaning of their caves and their persons.

But the mince of the Cider Lake country was never surpassed by any rival in tail-growing. He reigned supreme, proud in the knowledge that all beasts of prey must lick their chops in vain as they thought what succulent provender a plump and juicy mince would be. His homeland in the Saginaw was the true capital of the North Woods animal kingdom.

Naturally Paul Bunyan regarded the swigging mince as the greatest of game for the new invention, hunting.

"There can't be any meat for a thanksgiving meal like the meat of a mince," decided the great logger. "That's the stuff for the first hunting bag of history."

But another mighty creature had thought the same thing first. The great goebird of the North had been ravaging his way through the fauna of the forests all summer. He snapped tails wherever he flew. They were the primest provender for the goebird. Ere Paul Bunyan started his hunting trip, the goebird had wheeled thunderously out of the northern sky, narrowing his circling flight about the Cider Lake country until he had cleaned it up.

Only the foxes escaped. These cunning creatures thrust their tails down holes, sat on them, and pretended that they had no tails.

The first touch of winter darkened the sky as Paul and Babe reached the border of the mince country. The north wind had broken out with a bellowing blast and was heading for the Saginaw. Somber clouds rolled from his forefoot and heralded the approach of the storm king. The first harsh breeze stirred the trees of the lake lands. The woods lay black and wild under the bleak sky. All the sounds were dismal there. Gladness left the heart of Paul Bunyan as he hearkened to the tones that surged ominously from the deeps of the dark woods.

Whispering moans were merging with the sough of wind in the barren boughs. Certainly they were nothing but moans of sorrow, grief, and woe. Babe responded dolefully. The good ox sat back on his haunches, hoisted his muzzle, and mooed mournfully at the gray cloud packs. Now the woods wailed.

Paul Bunyan stood undecided, wondering and worrying. Now and again he caught familiar notes in the medley of moans and wails that surged out from the somber woods in the solemn wind. There was a racking sob—the shadow of the trumpeting voice of a bull moose, but his voice nevertheless. Here was a choked sob—was that a faint echo of the rabbit's raging roar? A stifled sob whispered out—and this was from a bereaved bear, no doubt. That hysterical sob could be only from an erstwhile happy doe. As he listened on, Paul Bunyan recognized all but one of the vast variety of sobs. The only kind lacking was the sob of joy. Now the logger heard the wind in the barren boughs as a dirge. The bleak sky was a pall. These were indeed funereal woods. But Paul Bunyan listened on.

Then his heart sank as he realized that one voice of the animal kingdom was unheard in the mourning. No matter how he strained his ears, he could hear no note that resembled the voice of the special game he was hunting. The gurgling mullow of the swigging mince had no echo or shadow here.

"I wonder," sighed Paul Bunyan forebodingly. "I wonder if the mince has been wiped out somehow. Maybe all the other timber beasts are mourning for the mince. What a shame if that should be! What would I say to the jacks, after promising them mince meat for a thanksgiving meal?"

He leaned on his scatter cannon, staring dismally into the wailing woods. It seemed too blasted bad, but the invention of hunting certainly looked to be a fizzle.

Then it happened.

Babe the Blue Ox suddenly rose from his haunches and instantly froze into a posture that was new for him. He extended his muzzle before him and his tail behind him until he had a perfectly straight line running from nose to tail brush, at the same time lifting his right front foot and crooking the leg. On his other three legs Babe stood as though carved from stone.

"Not trying to think, are you, Babe?" asked Paul.

Babe did not answer by even the twitch of an eyelash. Paul regarded the frozen ox quizzically. Never before had he seen the mercurial creature be so quiet and still.

"Something tremendous must be brewing up," worried the logger. "Wonder could it be an earthquake. Babe seems to be setting himself solid for something like that."

For once Paul Bunyan made a wrong guess. Hunting was so new to him that he did not realize that Babe was at heart a bird ox and had frozen into a point as he smelled one flying nigh. In the instant realization was forced upon him. Swooping down in his circling flight, the great goebird drove for Babe's extended tail, his wattles blazing like streaks of lightning, his beak snapping with a clanging thud like seventy-seven simultaneous ax-blows; and then he soared like a reversed shooting star to a vanishing-point. The likeness struck Paul Bunyan.

"A meteor, that's it," he murmured. "Hit Babe's tail and bounced skyhooting again—"

The great logger hushed that notion as he collected his wits. The absurdity of it was manifest when his logger's brains got to working again. Meteors never had feathers, and likewise they carried no snapping beaks along. Plainly and simply, this was certainly a ferocious fowl who could fly like thunder and strike like lightning. The plight of Babe gave Paul another cue. In another minute he was getting a grip on the actual situation.

The Blue Ox had broken his point. Twisting his neck, Babe stared with incredulous eyes at the root of his superb tail. It was already swelling there. The brush drooped to the ground. For the moment Babe could not hold it up. He glanced questioningly at Paul, then resumed his baffled stare at the swollen and paralyzed tail.

"You've been bit, Babe," explained Paul Bunyan kindly. "No wonder you can't believe it. If I hadn't seen it with my own eyes, I couldn't believe myself that anything alive could be brute enough to snap so vicious at that fine tail of yours. But some brute did."

The Blue Ox whimpered and moaned, then sat back on his haunches and began to lick the swollen spot. The sobs that emerged from the woods were a mystery no longer to Paul Bunyan. Certainly all the timber beasts had been despoiled of their tails by this ferocious fowl, and all were bemoaning their loss. Only its size had saved Babe's greatest pride from being sheared away. No doubt the fowl would try again.

The great logger was no longer a mere hunter after a bag of game. His disappointment over being deprived of mince meat was forgotten. He was sure that the ravager had done for all the monarchs of the lake lands. A living mince could not help but mullow, and not a mullow sounded now.

"Well, they're going to be revenged, by the bald-headed old Elisher and the brat-grabbing bears!" vowed Paul Bunyan, unlimbering his scatter cannon. "I don't mind losing a proper thanksgiving meal so pesky much, but the wiping out of the king tribe of timber beasts has got to be paid for in feathers and blood!"

Even as Paul roared the vow, a thunderous menacing growl rumbled up from the far horizon. At once Babe painfully curled his tail under his hind quarters and sat up, his forelegs dangling aloft, his eyes rolling in mute and fearful appeal at the feathered fury curving down the sky.

Seeing no tail, the fowl flew on without swooping. Nor did Paul Bunyan shoulder his scatter cannon and fire. It was plain that he could not hit such a lightning flyer with a straight shot. Curving on in its great circle, the goebird vanished again.

The hunter recognized the goebird on this trip. Many rumors had come to Quebec about this prehistoric fowl with the bronze feathers, red wattles, tail-snapping beak, and wheel tail. The spreading wheel tail was the source of the goebird's incredible speed. At its slowest the tail revolved like a windmill in a hurricane. Paul Bunyan had taken such rumors with a barrel of salt. But now he had to believe. At least one goebird survived, and one was enough to ruin all the game in the North Woods. Somehow he had to be brought down.

"He's flying on a curve, and so I got to shoot on a curve to get him now," reflected Paul Bunyan shrewdly.

Suiting the action to the word, he sprung the barrels of the scatter cannon over his knee until he judged that the shot would follow the curve of the goebird's flight. His sagacity now fully steamed up, Paul Bunyan in another instant invented the first decoy.

The idea was to make the goebird swoop and soar again, thus slowing his flight and bringing him close. Giant cat-tails were nodding near by, and Paul plucked one and swiftly thrust it into the ground at Babe's rear. Then Paul jerked at his beard. In a trice bits of whisker were adorning the decoy in such elegant style that Babe appeared to have sprouted suddenly the finest tail in the Saginaw timber.

"Here he comes," said Paul. "Shut your eyes, Babe, and set tight!"

The good ox seemed to understand. Again he proved what close communion existed between hunting ox and master. Not a muscle quivered under the silken blue coat as the goebird swooped with a guttural roar. The roar swelled into a note of triumph as the fowl soared with the false tail in its beak. For the instant of an instant the goebird hovered, and its roar was hushed.

The decoy fluttered downward. The deceit had been discovered.

Paul Bunyan fired. But even as the cannon-shot blazed from the thirty muzzles, the great bronze fowl was away. Its wheel tail was a fiery blur. Behind it the cannon-shot whistled and screamed, powder fogged up in storm clouds, the earth shook, and only sobs of fright sounded from the dark woods.

The hunter lowered his gun and stared hopefully through the smoke screen. The goebird was a curving streak, vanishing toward the horizon line as before. At its tail speeded the black cloud of cannon-shot. The gap between the speeding cloud and the curving bronze streak swiftly widened. Paul Bunyan set the stock of his scatter cannon on the ground, rested his hands on the muzzles, and bowed his head in defeat. Surely he had miserably failed.

Then Paul felt a warm, moist tongue licking his hand. He opened his eyes and tried to smile at his faithful hunting companion. Babe's eyes were two wet clouds of sympathy. But something more shone in them there.

Confidence, unquestioning, perfect, that was what. And there Babe's tail wagged in the same spirit. The faithful ox had forgotten his own hurt in the sympathy and confidence he felt so strongly.

Paul Bunyan's blood leaped and his voice roared.

"We'll bring him down yet, by the old slingshot of David!" the great hunter shouted, even as he saw the curving cannon-shot fall into the horizon line. "Got a gauge on the circle he's flying, anyhow. And now I know just how much to bend the barrels to shoot the goebird head on!"

Again he suited the action to the word. Hauling forth a fistful of cannon-shot and powder, he tamped a new charge home, straightened the barrels over his knee, then shrewdly bent them the other way, so that they would shoot the shot in a circle to meet the goebird's flight instead of following it.

He was just in time. Another rising roll of thunder announced that the goebird was curving up and on in his great circle from the horizon again. In an instant Paul Bunyan shouldered the scatter cannon, gauged windage and distance, and let fly with all thirty barrels. Then he dropped the stock from his shoulder, cradled the barrels in his left arm, held his breath, and stared with unblinking eyes.

Up the great circle curved the black cloud of cannon-shot, whistling and screeching as they flew. Down the great circle curved the great goebird, his raging roar announcing that this trip he would swoop to rend and tear whatever his beak and claws might reach, whether tails, noses, or ears. The cloud of cannon-shot loomed in his track. Paul Bunyan had gauged the circle truly and had bent the barrels right. The goebird had no time to soar or swerve. He tried a lightning dive. His wattled head darted down, then his mighty bronze back and wings, but he was just too late with his tail. The cannon-shot sheared it through, and the wind ballooned the swirling mass of tail feathers on down the Saginaw.

The goebird fell in a rainbow curve, his momentum bearing him on and on, tumbling him over and over, until at last he plunged earthward. It was as though a grand cloud bronzed by a sunset had suddenly swept down from the heavens.

Then that cloud seemed to be plunging into a surging blue lake as huge as itself. But this lake was actually Babe the Blue Ox leaping from his hind legs, his front hoofs waving, his jaws wide, teeth bared, a snarling moo vibrating from his throat. Cloud and lake collided. They vanished in a snowstorm of feathers. As Paul Bunyan ran up, Babe emerged from the storm. From his teeth dangled a wattled head. Babe had avenged his bitten tail.

The timber beasts were also avenged, for the goebird lost his head because he had lost them their tails. And now the avenger discovered a superb reward in his kill. The goebird was fat with the richest meat ever heard of, for he had fed on minces until even his raw drumsticks dripped. Grandly uplifted by this find, happy to know that the invention of hunting had exceeded all he had claimed for it, Paul Bunyan knew no bounds to his pride and joy. Here he had the game to make the best as well as the first thanksgiving meal of history.

It needed the broad back of Babe to carry the goebird to camp. He submitted proudly to the burden, having an instant change of heart. Babe was a hunting ox no longer. He was a tote ox now.

The procession down to the Big Onion was truly

triumphal. The tail feathers of the goebird had blown down along the trail, the quills driving into the earth. There they stood, waving like so many poplars as Paul and Babe marched by.

Also on the return trail the sun shone once more. All the dark clouds turned over, and their silver linings glittered down on the woods. But there was no light anywhere like that which shone in the eyes of Babe and Paul when they gazed in fond, rapt pride at one another.

"Good hunting," their bright glances said.

VII

THE SPRING OF THE
MUD RAIN

Now the weather was ready to make war on Paul Bunyan. Rivers had failed to resist his invasion of the Saginaw, but the weather had no doubt about itself. At last it had the seasons under discipline and in perfect marching order. Winter never missed a minute, but reported for duty every morning of its season. Snows fell, frost sheeted the lakes and rivers with ice, and the grand Round froze to a depth of eleven feet. Beyond the northern arch Shot Gunderson hoped in vain for six feet more. When spring broke and the whales came again, the battleship of a man was yet waiting for his chance to attack the boss logger.

Paul Bunyan was logging Big Sunny Valley this year. Mountainous banks of perfect pines towered above the smiling river. The ice went out. For another year, at least, Shot Gunderson would have to bide his time.

The camp lay in the fork of the Big Sunny and the Little Moon. On the eve of the drive the shanty boys turned in early. With nothing but confidence in his thoughts and kindness in his heart, Paul Bunyan sank into the private hill that he had padded for his comfort and warmth.

There was never a finer eventide. The light of the setting sun reddened out in a spotless spring sky. Not a hint was on the southern horizon of the baleful war clouds that the weather was rolling toward the Saginaw country. The camp slumbered in contentment. From every bunk shanty there was a flow of serenity in the endless chorus of snores.

The sun sank to rest. The pines sighed drowsily in the eventide breeze. The hours darkened on. For a moment the moon peered over the valley rim. Then it was blotted out. At midnight the sky to the south was smothered in a blackness of ponderous cloud packs. They sagged ever lower as they rolled sluggishly on. The breeze was hushed. Silence pervaded the timberlands. It was unbroken until the hour for dawn.

Babe the Blue Ox was the first to sound a warning of the black and soggy clouds massed by the weather for an attack on Paul Bunyan. This night Babe had gone to sleep as he stood at his manger, his head thrust through the open window of the stable, his chin resting on the sill. In such a posture Babe had enjoyed the bright sights and sweet sounds of the spring night until all lulled him into rare slumber.

At the hour for dawn the loudest moo of the Blue Ox suddenly thundered through the sleeping camp. There could be no mistake about the source of such a tremendous volume of sound. Only the loudest moo of Babe could toss the shanty boys from their bunks, turn them over three times, drop them back, and then neatly tuck their blankets about them all. When his blankets were tucked, every man jack knew what had happened.

"Babe's a mooin' his biggest and best!" was the yell that resounded from shanty to shanty. "Hang on for another bouncin' there!"

The jacks lay wide-eyed, holding their breaths, wondering what evil was threatening the camp.

Their Big Feller was already in action. Babe's moo could not lift, turn, and tuck such a mighty man as himself, of course, but the thunder of it had stirred him from sleep. At once Paul knew that dire trouble threatened. Babe was perfectly trained as a watch ox. When his voice blasted the night, danger was certain to be nigh.

The boss logger hastened so in his rush from the private padded hill that pines fell like weeds before his stride.

It was now considerably past the time for dawn to break, yet only the murkiest light filtered through the woods. Paul saw Babe's head as a vague shadow jutting from the stable window. The shadow was uttering small whimpering moos; and now Babe's bulging eyes were revealed as they rolled fearfully at the sky. Something struck his uplifted muzzle with a dull plopping sound. Babe's jaws spread to unloose another mighty moo of fright.

"Babe, you hush," ordered Paul sternly. "You'll give all the jacks rheumatism, bouncing and tucking them with your best and biggest moos like that. Babe, you hush your mouth there!"

The Blue Ox obediently shut his jaws, but he continued to breathe in windy moans. Paul Bunyan drew closer. He blinked incredulously; then his eyes glittered with amazement. The same emotion caused his beard to stiffen like pine boughs in a hurricane.

Babe's muzzle and head were spotted like a goebird's egg!

"He's sick," surmised Paul, after collecting his wits. "He's either got the chicken pox or the measles, by the old miseries of Job!" Then he reflected more calmly, his sagacity seizing the situation. "Johnny Inkslinger can shave the chicken pox off, but measles go deeper. Measles have got to be dug or blasted out when they sink their spots into man or beast. No other way to cure measles, so I do hope it ain't them Babe has got."

Hoping fervently for the best, Paul yelled for Johnny Inkslinger to come with his first-aid outfit.

"Fetch the razor you use to shave the chicken pox off the shanty boys, too, Johnny!" ordered Paul. "The razor and the lather!"

While he waited for the great doctor and figurer, Paul Bunyan began to hear ominous sounds. They came from the murky shadows of the pines.

Drip-drip-drip.

Plop-plop-plop.

Such queer sounds came to the quivering ears of Paul Bunyan. He peered curiously through the murk, staring down on the pines, stooping as he stared. The tallest of these trees reached hardly to the great logger's short ribs.

Paul Bunyan stared down at the trees, and now he perceived that all were a dead black. Not a sprig of green showed, but black and dripping and plopping were all the trees. And the sky was black and low all over and around. The sun should be rising soon, he thought, yet the murk was not lightening. A qualm struck Paul Bunyan. Another instantly followed. As Paul straightened up he was smitten by a whole swarm of qualms. Never before had he seen such April morning shower clouds. Never before had he felt such drops of April rain on his face.

The raindrops stuck. That was the queer thing about them all. They stuck to his nose, to his cheeks, to his ears, to his eyes; and to his beard, which still jutted stiffly like pine boughs, the raindrops stuck in round black spots.

Now Paul Bunyan began to understand the fear that had made Babe burst forth in his loudest moo. He knew what the baleful cloud packs portended. His fear that Babe had broken out with the measles dwindled to nothing. An incomparably mightier menace than measles was in the air.

"It's war," affirmed Paul Bunyan solemnly. "The weather has declared war on me here, turning the Saginaw from a logging land into a battle ground. Well, so be it. If the weather wants war, that's what it'll get, by the hairy old fists of Samson and the jawbone of the ass!"

To understand the martial passion of Paul Bunyan it must be remembered that in the old Quebec country the weather had always co-operated peacefully in the grand life of getting out the logs. There the mildest clouds would never spill showers on the boss logger, but always parted before his path.

The weather here was just the reverse, it appeared. Regular rain Paul Bunyan could bear with a tolerant spirit. But a mud rain would gum up the rivers for log driving. Only to defend the life he had invented for the woods did Paul Bunyan square off defiantly at the black cloud packs.

Then galloping footsteps sounded nigh.

Dr. Johnny Inkslinger was answering the call of duty. The famous man of pills and figures galloped up, his eyes bulging a foot above the rims of his square spectacles, the rubber eraser worn always on the tip of his long nose bobbing with agitation. Johnny skidded to a halt before Paul Bunyan.

Then he yelled: "Mr. Bunyan, you're all broke out!" He bowed feverishly, never forgetting to be polite. "Have you got a rash? Been eating strawberries, Mr. Bunyan?"

"No, Johnny," said Paul grimly. "It's just that the weather has declared war on me. I certainly wish it was the measles or a strawberry rash, but it's not. War, Johnny, that's the trouble."

"It can't be, Mr. Bunyan," said Inkslinger, respectful but firm. "I got it down in black and white that the weather is bound to keep the peace."

"Two acts of war," asserted the boss logger. "*Imprimis*, the weather has rained on me. *Imprimis* number two, the weather's raining mud. If that ain't war, I'd like to know what is, by the weeping old Jeremiah!"

Johnny held out his palm. It was instantly spattered

and spotted. He smelled the spots, then tasted seven or eight, and at last nodded in agreement.

"Mud, Mr. Bunyan," he agreed. Then the timekeeper assumed a cheerful outlook. "But I wouldn't say a mud rain meant war. Why, I figger a mud rain'll be interesting. I'll kind of enjoy a change from a regular rain myself, Mr. Bunyan."

"Johnny," said the boss logger solemnly, "do you realize that the rivers'll be running mud instead of water? Why, I'm already changing the name of the Big Sunny to the Big Muddy and that of the Little Moon to the Little Sloppy. Well, if it ain't a battle to make a log drive down a mud river, what would you call it? Nothing else. It's war with the weather if I make this drive, and you can't argue around it, Johnny."

"You'll make the drive, Mr. Bunyan!" Johnny Inkslinger's voice rang with proud faith. "You would never let a spring go by without making a log drive. That's why you're boss logger of the North woods, Mr. Bunyan!"

Paul soberly nodded. He knew that the least of his jacks expected him to pull off a drive every spring, no matter what obstacles appeared. To keep the grand life of logging going as he had started it, he had to wage a winning war against the weather, even as he had royally resisted rebellious rivers. For the latter, muscle had been mighty enough. The weather, however, did not own a nature that could be subdued by fist and boot.

"Nothing but sagacity can win this here war," said Paul, facing facts. "Got to call all my sagacity into play, or into fight, I mean."

He brooded over the situation, stroking his now relaxed beard, grimly ignoring the thickening spots of
mud rain on his person. Johnny Inkslinger stood respectfully by. Then Hels Helson roared up. He was
jubilant.

"Bay yee, Ay feel so gude noo!" roared Hels. "Oh,
Ay like this mud rain har! Ay don' gat vash foor one
year, Ay bat you!"

The boss logger did not hear his foreman. Already
his mind was deep in a plan for a defense against the
weather. Paul Bunyan strode to his private padded
hill. For five days and nights he sat there, brushing his
beard with a pine tree, now and then shaking the mud
from his shoulders or poking it from behind his ears, his
sheltered sagacity searching for a means to drive logs
down a river running with mud.

In the meanwhile the black clouds rolled ever on,
and from them nothing but mud dripped, showered and
poured.

"She's rainin' mud cats and mud dogs," the shanty
boys complained. "It's all up and off with loggin' in
the Saginaw. The Big Feller'll never make a drive this
trip. And once the weather gets him licked, it'll blow up
a mud rain ever' spring, you betcher!"

They could hardly be blamed for becoming shanty
boys of little faith. The pines were coated and caked
with mud. The birds and beasts of the timber were
plastered. The golden waters of the Big Sunny were no
more, and the Little Moon no longer shone with silvery gleams from dawn glow to eventide. Their waters

thickened. The old names of the streams were left to history. The Big Muddy and the Little Sloppy now oozed on to Saginaw Bay, the playground of the Round River whales.

A funereal quiet descended on the great camp. It was broken only by the endless plop-plop-plop of the falling mud drops and the dismal drip-drip-drip from the burdened pines. The idle jacks stared morbidly from the shanty doors, their hearts sinking hour by hour. In vain Johnny Inkslinger attempted to buoy their spirits up.

"Come on, fellows!" he would cry cheerily. "It's always darkest before the dawn! The blackest clouds have silver linings! Look on the bright side! Come on, fellows, let's repeat the Shanty Boys' Creed!"

Even in their best times the shanty boys gagged at the creed Johnny Inkslinger had rigged up for them, and now they only scowled and sneered. The timekeeper had to give them up. Fortunately he had figures, first-aid incantations, and woodcraft rigmarole with which to occupy himself. At last he left the lads to their grouches.

In their dour situation the jacks felt the spirit of men working in them again. They bitterly recalled King Pete's promises of the Year of the Good Old Times for the Saginaw timber country.

"These look like 'em, don't they, hey?" the jacks sneered.

They remembered the days when they were Wild Irish, Terrible Swedes, Hairy Scotch, and Fighting French in Europe, and a few of the crankiest began to argue politics. Brawls ensued. More and more Paul

Bunyan's jacks began to behave like the men they used to be. This was all to the bad. But it was ever so when the grand life of logging was halted for any reason. Then the jacks would resume their human nature. On the other hand, they got along as decently as well-behaved bears while logging went on. Now, as they argued and glowered, the shanty boys showed how human they were at heart.

"Sweden be blasted!" bawled the Wild Irish.

"Fooey foor Ireland!" snorted the Terrible Swedes.

The French and Scotch took to whisker-pulling and shin-kicking on account of politics. Certainly bears would have been astonished by such violent human nonsense. But the jacks were not to blame. It was all the fault of the weather.

Not a rift appeared in the coal-black sky. But for their dripping moisture, the pines had the look of snags left from a forest fire. Mud sheathed the log banks on the rollways. Night was a time of impenetrable darkness. Every day was a damp, gloomy shadow. Ruin was clouding down on the Saginaw.

Even Hels Helson was not so happy now. He was stuck in the mud at last. Not with his feet, which were superb mud-boats, but with his hands. Attempting a prodigious chew of snoose, mud had rained into the absorbent ore, thickening it into a molasses-like mass. The stuff would cling like glue to the Big Swede's left hand, for example; he would pull it free with his right; and naturally his right hand would then be gummed with the sticky stuff.

Soon the molasses-like ball had Hels completely

addled. Seated in the shelter of Babe's stable, the Swede spent weary hours pulling the ball from first one hand and then the other. At night he would succumb to sleep, but in the morning he would stubbornly tackle the perplexing chore again. Babe was neglected and began to protest with doleful moos. The Blue Ox was missing the evening romps and frolics he had enjoyed with the buck whales of Saginaw Bay while the spring was still smiling.

It was Babe who finally showed the way to Paul Bunyan. On the fifth morning of the mud rain the bored ox could no longer bear the monotony of the black season. He kicked open the stable door and, with a defiant flourish of his tail, headed through the dark, gummy rain for the shore of Saginaw Bay.

Paul saw the Blue Ox go. He started a command for Babe's return, then choked it down. In the instant his sagacity had heaved out the idea for a winning battle against the weather.

Paul Bunyan rose up, shaking off layers of mud like blankets. Now he marched for the inexhaustible storehouse and bundled up a shoulder-load of leather, hewing-tools, and his old Quebec fishing-net. But once he paused to reassure his men.

"It's all going to come out in the wash," he said.

The saying was invented just in time to halt a political riot. Now all the men remembered that they were jacks. Their hearts throbbed in unison with the hope of pulling off the most famous drive since the Big Auger one. It was one band of bullies, one bunch of timber savages, that repeated Paul Bunyan's affirmation.

"She's all comin' out in the wash, you betcher!" the shanty boys said. "Hurray fer the Big Feller!"

In another moment Paul Bunyan had vanished down the river trail. Overhead the clouds thickened. The mud fell in sheets. **War was on in earnest.**

VIII

WHY THE GREAT LAKES HAVE NO WHALES

THE weather was charging in a column of clouds. This was evident to the boss logger as he approached Saginaw Bay. Here the clouds thinned toward the eastern horizon. More light filtered through, and the raindrops ran. The waters of the bay itself were unthickened. Yet enough mud had poured in from the big river to prove that it was not a disagreeable element for whales. The whole host of bucks disported frolicsomely as Babe the Blue Ox played pitch and fetch with them, showing that the mud rain had not dampened their spirits in the least.

"I knowed it," said Paul triumphantly to himself. "The deep-water kin of carps, that's what whales are. And they'll tame to the halter just as easy as carps do, that's what I'll bet, by the old hospitality of the great fish of Jonah!"

Hope surged on in the boss logger's heart as he watched Babe swing a pine tree in his jaws and pitch it far over the bay. The buck whales spouted and leaped under the arc of the flying pine, butting each other with thunderous thuds, their eyes shining with eagerness and excitement. None of the other whales displayed resentment or envy when the victor in the race fetched the tree back to Babe to pitch again.

"Just as kind and friendly as they were in Jonah's time, whales are," Paul Bunyan thought on, his sublime idea striking deeper than ever in his mind. "Let me handle 'em right, and they'll take to log driving like they were born to it."

It was not yet the time for whale-taming, however. This first day had to be devoted to preparations. Skirting the shore until the bank of Round River was reached, Paul then unshouldered the great net and stretched it across the mouth of the bay. Now he had a stout whale-pen, from which there could be no escape. The inspired boss logger then spent the rest of the day working the leather from the stores into enormous bridles and saddle girths, and in hewing pines into the form of pack-saddle crosstrees. At nightfall he counted his sets and then took a census of the bucks in his impromptu whale-pen.

"One outfit apiece, and fifty-nine left over for extras," concluded the boss logger, with a sigh of satisfaction. "Tomorrow I start to tame 'em down and break 'em in."

He called Babe, who was yet unwearied from the long day of pitching pines a mile. The buck whales now noticed the logger. They observed him with suspicion and backed timidly from the shore. But Paul Bunyan was sure that he could lull all their doubts. Even now the whales saw that their playmate trusted him implicitly. This was already a strong point in his favor. In the camp stores was stuff which should entirely win their trust. Paul thanked his lucky stars for Snoose Mountain. It was his sagacious surmise that the magic ore would be a treat for whales.

"The Big Swede," reasoned Paul, "is a fish-eater and a snoose-lover. Whales also eat fish. Ergo, whales should also love snoose. The Blue Ox, on the other hand, is herbivorous, and snoose is not native to his nature. Yet he enjoys playing with whales even as he does with Hels. All in all, I vow that these whales here are more like a Swede than an ox. They'll be eating out of my hand tomorrow."

With that botanical boast, Paul Bunyan clucked at Babe. Hero and ox vanished in the deep shadows of the thick clouds up river. The buck whales wallowed and drowsed, waiting for the murky morning to bring their playfellow again.

Again the sun had risen unseen. Paul Bunyan labored to break whales to the bridle and pack-saddle. His method had been thought out shrewdly during the night. In the taming he must soften firmness with kindness, and in the breaking he must toughen kindness with firmness again. Softly, shrewdly, firmly, kindly, toughly, he proceeded from buck to buck, day after day, ignoring the downpour from the apparently limitless reserves of mud clouds, tempering each of the friendly-spirited mammals to his purpose.

For kindness Paul would woo one of the shy and suspicious creatures with a hogshead of snoose, holding it out betwixt a thumb and forefinger, and coaxing in a fine tone.

"Come on, buck. Come, boy, now," Paul would wheedle, his voice murmuring as gently through his beard as a spring breeze through green grass. "Come, boy. Co'! Co'! Hopsy daisy! There's the whale. Co', lad. Come, boy. Wrap your lips around this snoose here. There's a dozy lad! That's being a whale, buck!"

Slowly and gingerly the shy young buck whale would swim toward the ingratiating logger; halting now and again, wriggling his flukes, hoisting his snout above the water and cocking one questioning eye at Paul Bunyan; then the whale would get one salty and peppery sniff of the powerful panacea; and his tongue would loll out, fairly streaming with his hunger for the barreled hundredweight of the rarest delicacy known to whales and Swedes. His mouth watering more and more, the buck whale would edge closer, on and on, and finally he would cast off all restraint and boldly leap to grab the dainty with one snap of his jaws.

As the whale snapped, a bridle would be slipped like lightning over his head, and a pine-tree bit would be thrust between his snapping jaws. But now this mattered nothing to the buck. For an hour he would be quivering only from the ravishing emotions that coursed from the hundred pounds of snoose wadded in his cheek. Paul Bunyan's sagacity had reasoned aright. The whales and the Big Swede were brothers under their hides.

At last all the buck whales were wooed and won by the kindness of Paul Bunyan. Now he needed to call firmness into play. Time pressed. Day followed day as bee follows bee in hiving-time. Steadily the black battalions of the weather rolled on. And just as steadily the Big Muddy thickened. Back in camp the shanty boys were once more reverting to a state of human nature. If the weather won, they might never be fit for logging again. So Paul Bunyan hastened.

In his haste he was sometimes harsh with the whales. More than one felt the lash of the whale whip when he reared rebelliously under the trees of the pack-saddle or balked against the pull of the bridle reins, his eyes glittering stubbornly from the shadows of the blinders. Then the lash would fall, and the whale would be forced into sullen submission. Most of the punished bucks could be mollified with snoose. Only a few were natural outlaws and trouble-makers, remaining sullen and stubborn to the end.

Eventually every whale was at least outwardly tractable. Paul Bunyan, with a sigh of weariness and relief, tied his new work-whales together and started up river for the rollways.

The boss logger tramped the river trail, a rope woven and spliced from young pine trees swinging from his hands. At the other end of the rope the most snoose-loving and kind-tempered bucks led the herd. They swam with laborious energy against the current of mud, the less tractable bucks following in fair order. The outlaws were kept in line by Babe, who would dash into the river and snap at the flukes of any buck who tried to start a stampede. The Blue Ox was the playfellow of whales no longer. He was all business when it came to getting out the logs. So discipline was maintained. By nightfall the whales were all tethered up river from the rollways.

Babe remained on watch. Paul Bunyan retired for a bit of rest in his private hill. The drive should start at dawn.

An hour before the time for dawnbreak the shanty boys heard the Big Feller's voice rolling through the shadows.

"Roll out or roll up! It's down the river, men!"

Every jack grumbled from his blankets as he heard the old driving call. In each shanty the embers on the open camboose fireplace glowed a deep red. Not a ray from the sky touched the square smoke-hole in the roof. The drops of mud rain spattered down, hissing on the embers as they baked dry.

"The Big Feller's waited too long," the jacks complained. "It'll simply be bog and sink with the logs now. This here's one spring he won't make a drive. Ol' Paul seems to be losin' his holt."

Paul Bunyan smiled grimly through his beard as he heard the growling and grumbling from the shanties. He was entirely tolerant of it all. It had been a miserable wait. The weather had to bear all the blame. The men would be his bully jacks again as soon as they learned what a famous drive was in store. Just as soon as they saw that they were to ride and drive whales this morning, the men would realize that everything had indeed come out in the wash.

Paul Bunyan let the news wait. The jacks were still

growling and grumbling as they started for the rollways in the dim light of dawn.

This was the sorriest-looking gang of woodsmen that ever marched a river trail. Every jack was mud-caked, from the tassel of his cap to the spikes of his boots. Mackinaws were stiff and drab. All beards were stiff and black. The men moved in a shambling march, now and again breaking into a goosestep to shake the mud from their boots. They dragged their peaveys, their shoulders slumped, their eyes fixed in dull, dismal stares at the muddy trail.

Paul Bunyan marched in the lead. His head was up, his cap seeming to touch the lowering clouds. Beside him labored Johnny Inkslinger, the logarithms which he used in scaling logs shielded by a vast umbrella attached to his figuring pencil. Hels Helson tramped blindly, entirely occupied with the gluey ball of snoose and mud that yet persisted in clinging to one or the other of his hands. From up the river sounded an eager moo of welcome.

To the right of the trail the pines wearily dripped and plopped from the mud rain pouring ever and anon from the sky. Their black boughs sagged, too burdened to stir in the hardest wind. Mud puddles spotted the forest floor. The creeks gurgled with thick, heaving floods. The Big Muddy oozed on in a sluggish current, its body soggy and dark. The clouds rolled dolorously.

Paul Bunyan led the march past the rollways. When he called a halt, his men were still slumped and staring dismally at the trail. They looked up sullenly as the boss logger roared:

"Seventeen peavey men to each rollway there! All others take to the whales! One jack to a buck! Mount whales, men! For the first time in history we're driving logs down a mud river! For the first time in botany we're driving logs with whales! Boots and saddles and charge, by the four hossback riders of the old Apocalipsy!"

For the second time this morning the boss logger of the North Woods smiled through his beard at his shanty boys. This time it was not a grim smile, but proud and fond. Here in the grand old Saginaw timber country the men had grown to be true jacks at heart. They were showing it now. Give them something they could get a grip on, and all would keep the faith.

Certainly there was nothing bigger for the jacks to get a grip on than whales. And how they were taking hold! At first they were smitten blank with amazement at seeing a huge herd of whales tethered along the river bank, each one humped under a pack-saddle, champing a bit, and staring out from bridle blinders. But all the jacks quickly recovered. Their hearts thumped and the hair on their chests stiffened valiantly as the Big Feller roared them on:

"Mount whales, men! Ride 'em handsome and high!"

Forgetting fears and doubts and all other particles of human nature, the jacks swarmed down the river banks, picked mounts, and swung boldly up. Some trouble ensued. Here an outlaw took the bit in his teeth and charged off in a runaway down river, his rider vainly tugging at the reins, until Babe floundered out, his jaws snapping as he herded the outlaw back into line. There another outlaw lunged, bucking blindly up river, heaving his rider in convulsive jumps, until the lash of Paul Bunyan's whale whip quoiled him down. Several such scenes were enacted in the river of mud.

But at last the columns were formed in good order. Hogsheads of snoose were passed round. The whales settled down. Even the outlaws munched in apparent resignation. Atop his mount every proud jack stared at his neighbor with shining eyes. And now this yell rolled along the river:

"You can't stop the Big Feller from pulling off a spring drive! Not even a mud rain can beat him, you betcher!"

The worst was indeed over. The only other threat of trouble was from a troop of calves which had followed the herd up from the whale-pen. The calves found the Big Swede standing knee-deep in the stream, still addled over his snoose and mud ball. The calves decided to play leapfrog with Hels, so they charged his legs and knocked him down. Then they discovered that by butting him in the ribs they could tickle him into convulsions. Hels rolled and laughed helplessly, downing barrels of mud every time he opened his cavernous mouth, until Paul tossed some snoose downstream. The calves rushed away to chase snoose, and Hels was saved. In the turmoil he had wiped the perplexing sticky ball on his shirt, so now he was free of it and ready to break out the rollways.

Hels Helson stood at ready where the mud river

surged along the rollways. Johnny Inkslinger opened his logarithms, his umbrella pencil shedding the drops of mud rain. The peavey men poised their tools. The first whale, a huge, docile buck, was halted in place for loading.

"Timber!" roared Paul Bunyan. "Let 'er roll!"

The river roared back at him as the log banks broke. The peavey men swarmed the heaving slopes of tumbling logs like grasshoppers. Down at the bottom the Big Swede scooped the timbers in his cleaned paws and stacked them high in the pack-saddle trees, binding the tiers. Above the back of each whale towered a pyramid of logs. On the top log, the binder, crouched the jack in charge; his arms stiff, his hands steady as he gripped the reins slanting down to the bit in the jaws of his whale mount. So the first column of whales moved ponderously on in the mud river.

In an hour a squadron was lined up in ranks, four abreast. The whales rested at ease, heaving in the sluggish swells of the stream. Paul Bunyan kept his whale whip uncoiled, but he was to swing its lash no more. Even the outlaws held an unbroken formation, as squadron after squadron fell into line. At last the boss logger stared at emptied rollways.

"Down the river!" commanded Paul Bunyan.

The river thundered and boiled from threshing flukes.

"Yay, whales!" bawled the jacks.

The drive was on.

On in a huge sweep swam the buck whales, bearing the logs irresistibly down the muddy tide and round the first big bend. A cheer burst from the deeps of Paul Bunyan's heart for the magnificent sight. His pride in his shanty boys knew no bounds now. The purpose and the plan had been his, but the fulfillment was theirs. For once his distrust of the human nature inherent in all men was smothered.

There they stood, genuine timber savages, true bullies of the woods! Down the river and round the bend the jacks drove the logs on the backs of whales! Every jack kept his calks set solidly in the top log of his pyramid, sprung his knees, hunched shoulders, clenched his fists, and solidly held a tight rein. The snouts of the whales were up, their jaws gaped as they fought the bit; and as they lunged through the sucking and dragging mud at blinding speeds, their drivers bravely yelled:

"Yay, whales! Show 'em all the colors of your flukes there!"

So the drive rounded the big bend. Paul Bunyan cut through the timber to beat the drive to the river's mouth. The rest was easy, the battle was won. In the bay he would unload the logs, boom them, and then set the whales free. The great logger was content. In this first encounter he had licked the weather even as he had beaten the wild young rivers. This day Paul Bunyan had made history, and botany as well.

But one eventuality marred Paul Bunyan's triumph. In never another spring did the whale herds swim up from deep salt water and jump Niagara to use Round River as a calving- and nursing-ground. The bridle, the bit, the blinders, the pack-saddle, and the whale whip were bitter memories to all the bucks. Even the ones who were urged to return by fond recollections of snoose and of playing pitch and fetch with Babe considered that Paul Bunyan had taken advantage of the hospitable and friendly nature of whales, so famous since Jonah's time. The outlaws were utterly intolerant. They refused to believe that Paul Bunyan might receive them differently in fine weather.

Thus the Great Lakes, the mighty sons of Round River, Father of Waters, remain barren of whales to this day.

For the lamentable lack Paul Bunyan may be blamed. But who can find the heart to blame him? He had to whip the weather. He had to get out the logs.

IX

LITTLE FRAID AND BIG SKEERY

PAUL BUNYAN had learned to expect anything in the old Saginaw; but a river so timorous, fearful, skittish and shy as to be scared of its own shadow was certainly the least of his expectations. Nevertheless, he found two such rivers as he logged north, after the spring of the Mud Rain.

In the autumn Paul established camp in the fork of the Little Fraid and Big Skeery. The main stream emptied into Thunder Bay, a violent fighting arm of Round River. The bay was a favorite haunt of the weather when out on a big blow. Then wind and water would roar and tussle like mad. The blows were so frequent and so terrifying that the bay's main tributary had been wind-beaten into a stream as cowardly and cringing as the Big Auger had been belligerent and bold. When Paul Bunyan saw the cowering and trembling river, he was indignant.

"Who in tarnation did this here to you?" roared Paul. "Whoever it was, just let me lay a paw on him once! It's right and proper to give a river the discipline it needs," he went on, more calmly, "but anybody who bullies and abuses a river ought to be broke in two. Just let him show himself and I'll crack him, by the old Eden and Bethesda!"

Of course the river did not reply. But the weather heard, and muttered dourly over the bay, which heaved in sullen swells. The weather was not yet ready for another battle, however. The mud rain had left it generally exhausted and disheartened. So the weather was taking it easy with its regular autumn and winter work. In the east, wind power was gathering for the purpose of roaring over in the spring and battering back the next log drive. But the weather was keeping this purpose concealed.

The Big Skeery flowed on, now slowly and timidly, now in a mad panic of fear. The river was out of the question for log driving in its present condition. In its timid stretches the river hardly moved, but lay in dark, shivering pools. Here a log drive would move hardly a mile in seven days. In its panicky stretches the river was a wild welter of foam, surging and plunging in crazy whirlpools, backing furiously, then boiling madly on, until a timid stretch was reached. In such places a log drive would move at the rate of seventy miles an hour and be battered into slivers.

Here indeed was a baffling problem for the boss logger of the North Woods. His muscle could not matter a whit in solving it. Here Paul Bunyan had to be all sagacity.

The Little Fraid was even worse than the Big Skeery. The branch had numerous caverns under its bed, into which it could run and hide when the weather and water were having a rowdy blow down on Thunder Bay. When Paul Bunyan approached the Little Fraid, the stream at once ran for cover. He did not get a glimpse of it until he pretended to turn his back on the deserted river bed. Then he suddenly wheeled round. The river was peeking out shyly from under its bed. It was a pretty, silvery stream, and Paul smiled and clucked at it with cheery friendliness. Nevertheless, the river vanished.

"It's going to take a pile of coaxing, the Little Fraid is," reflected Paul Bunyan, as he tramped back to camp. He thought on. "Wonder if the funny little cuss of a river ain't been starved a lot." The idea appeared to have something to it, as Paul worked it over. "Snow-starved, that's the trouble with the Little Fraid, I bet. Give it a plenty of snow for once, and it ought to quit playing hide-and-go-seek and run like a regular river. I'll take a whirl at the idea anyhow, by the water-spouting rock of Moses!"

The weather heard, and its autumn breezes snarled through the pine boughs.

But much more than a huge feed of snow would be necessary to transform the Big Skeery into a sturdy, steady, courageous, self-reliant river of the North Woods. Tramping back to camp, Paul Bunyan saw Hels Helson dipping Babe's water-bucket into one of the stream's trembling pools. The simple and honest purpose of Hels was to fetch Babe a cool drink. Filling the water-bucket would lower the river no more than a foot, and that only for the time being. But the Big Skeery evidently feared it would be entirely emptied.

Suddenly the quiet pool began to foam. It backed away in terror from Hels Helson. He was stooped far over the river, ready to dip, and as the pool dodged him, he toppled head foremost into the now panic-stricken stream. Above the turbulent and turbid river his legs kicked wildly. Mud bubbles the size of balloons floated up amid the foam and spray. Now the river lost itself in an utter frenzy of fear. It parted in the middle from Hels, leaving him marooned in a mudhole island, and washing out a new channel on each side of him.

The Big Swede was buried to his hips. Only his legs showed above the mudhole as the panicky river raged on in its new channels. Its bed quaked from the stifled heaves of Hels. Paul Bunyan hastened to camp. There he shouldered his old Quebec fishing-net with one hand and yoked Babe with the other. The logger and the ox then made for the river bank in a gallop. In a twinkling the net was swung over the Big Swede's boots. They were rapidly vanishing, as every effort Hels made to free himself only buried him the more. Babe was hitched to the net, and he bellied down for a hard pull. Hels popped out like a cork from a bottle. Plastered and dripping, spewing geysers of mud with every breath, he was eased down on the bank by Paul Bunyan.

"Cheer up, Hels!" the boss logger consoled his foreman. "You've just made some geography for yourself. Out there where you were stuck is the only hole island known to geography."

The Big Swede raised up feebly and tried to look.

Sure enough, the river was still shying two ways round the hole in the mud. There it was, a regular hole, and yet an island because it was entirely surrounded by water.

Hels Helson attempted a feeble smile of pride. Instantly it vanished. Johnny Inkslinger was bounding down from the camp office to render first aid. Hels roared up to escape with all his powers. At that the river began to shiver and run wild again. Paul Bunyan's voice rolled commandingly over the scene.

"To the rear, Johnny! March, there!" The charging timekeeper whirled on the balls of his feet at the command. The new direction headed him for Babe's stable. With the urge aroused, Johnny had to give first aid to somebody, so he tackled the Blue Ox, who snoozed serenely on through the entire ceremony. "Take to cover, Hels!" the boss logger's command roared on from the river. "You got to keep away from the Big Skeery here! The sight of you sets the river wild. Take cover there, Hels!"

"Ay do it, you bat you," growled the Big Swede. "Bay yee, Ay don' like rivers anyhoo. Rivers vas too vet, yesiree!"

All autumn and winter Hels Helson was careful to keep away from the Big Skeery. His winter's job was to fill the valley of the Little Fraid with snow, from rim to rim. Hels did not mind this task. The shy little stream kept entirely underground as its frozen bed was covered with snow from the Big Swede's scoop, and the packing of its valley continued. Hels Helson developed a fondness for the Little Fraid. He would like all rivers, he thought, if all rivers would only stay underground like this one.

Logging went serenely on. Paul Bunyan prepared a new private padded hill for himself as the chopping season progressed and the first snows fell. His sagacity always demanded such a seat for proper pondering. Upholstering a hill was no trick at all for Paul Bunyan.

First he stripped the sod of its trees. Then he skinned off the sod and laid it out like blankets spread for an airing. Next Paul Bunyan dug a deep hollow in the stripped hill, one with enough width to make a roomy seat for him. The bottom and sides were then lined with bushy pine boughs. This done, the sod blankets were replaced, stretched tautly over the padding, and pegged down with trimmed and polished trees. Seated in his private padded hill, Paul Bunyan would invariably think up potent notions. The hill above the Big Skeery worked perfectly as Paul pondered out a system for making an upstanding, self-respecting, self-reliant, log-running stream out of this meek and cringing coward of a river.

"Even a worm will turn," reasoned Paul Bunyan, as his sagacity began to get in its work. "And if a worm will, why won't a river? I claim a river will, and I aim to prove it. I'm going to goad the weather and the bay into putting up their savagest battle. Then the Big Skeery will be cornered up until its back is against the wall, and it will have to turn and fight or else die into a lake."

Paul Bunyan knew that lakes are rivers which have died. He hated to see a river pass away into a lake, but he was ready to take the risk. Anything would be better for a river than the timid and fearful life of the Big Skeery. And there was a fair chance that the river would turn when driven to the wall.

So the boss logger proceeded with his plan. Regular autumn rains fell, then regular winter snows blew down. The frost left ice on Round River as it skimmed down from the north. Thunder Bay froze solid. On the ice the wind piled snow in mountainous drifts. So the weather went on with its ordinary winter work.

Paul Bunyan was not letting the work alone, however. From the bay ice and from the hill slopes Hels Helson scooped snow and filled the valley of the Little Fraid. The weather raged impotently at such presumption, and it snowed in vain on the bare spaces. Hels was not to be denied as a snow-scooper. As each section of the little valley was filled to its rims, Paul proceeded with another part of his carefully laid plans. The dead boughs and the swamped bush from the clearings and skid trails were hauled by Babe to Little Fraid Valley, and Hels heaped them in a black ridge atop the snow bank. Slowly the valley was being transformed into a ridge of brush hills. The weather seemed to wonder at that. Paul Bunyan kept his own counsel. He had other tricks up his mighty sleeve.

As the winter went on, the boss logger did everything he could think of to infuriate his adversary beyond endurance. He taught Babe to suck the lowest-hanging clouds out of the sky and swallow them for drinking-water. One night Paul scattered snoose over the surface of Thunder Bay, and by dawn the fiery mineral had set the ice on fire. The weather had to work overtime for a week to snow the fire out and freeze the bay properly again. Then Paul Bunyan mixed the potent ore with blasting powder, and he fired blasts which made a rainstorm out of a blizzard with which the weather had toiled for a month, bringing it laboriously down from the north.

A thousand other infuriating and tormenting tricks Paul played on the weather before winter was done. When the north wind blew no more, the boss logger shrewdly guessed that the weather was saving it for a tremendous attack next winter. He did not worry.

"Time enough to worry when the norther blows," said Paul Bunyan. "Right now all I care about is for the Big Skeery to turn into a bully he-river fit for a spring drive."

All winter he and his men modeled their behavior with the sole idea of winning the confidence of the broken-spirited stream. The logs skidded to the banking-grounds by the Blue Ox were all padded so they could be rolled into position quietly and not frighten the river with loud sounds. Twenty times a day Paul Bunyan made it a point to speak kind and encouraging words to the Big Skeery, urging it to regard him as a friend. Babe entered into the spirit of the affair and frequently tried to lick the river as he did Paul's neck. But the Big Skeery always quivered as the huge red tongue of the Blue Ox descended toward it.

"To heel, Babe," Paul would kindly command. "The

river don't understand. It has never had any friendly kindness in its life. It thinks you're going to drink it up, the river does."

He knew that a river so beaten down could not be transformed in a season by kindness alone. It needed to be driven into a position in which it would have to make a fight for life.

"Then it will be sink or swim for this here river," said Paul Bunyan sagely. "I'm betting it's swim."

Of course the main reason for the boss logger's subtle strategy was his one great purpose of getting out the logs and bringing down a spring drive. If the Big Skeery, goaded into desperation, turned on the weather and won, it would remember Paul Bunyan as its friend and be proud to bear his log drive on. So he took such pains to show friendship for the frightened stream, even as he did everything to make the weather start a fight.

By spring the weather was goaded into a fierce fighting humor. It had been ready to rest and recuperate from the arduous business of the mud rain, holding its winds in reserve for a new attack next winter. But now the weather could not wait. It melted the ice and poured the fire of the sun into the snow. With the breaking of the first April dawn the weather charged. The advance blasts of the east wind beat into Thunder Bay and heaved giant waves into the mouth of the Big Skeery.

"All right. *Now* bring your drive down," the weather seemed to sneer.

Paul Bunyan ordered his jacks to keep to the shanties, resting on their peaveys, their driving boots laced, all ready to make instantly for the banking-grounds upon command. Johnny Inkslinger was posted to keep watch over Hels Helson. The foreman was to be the human means of making the first test on the river.

Paul himself tramped to the river bank and stood guard. He leaned guard, rather, as the force of the wind from Thunder Bay was hard enough to topple even such a mighty man as himself. Paul Bunyan kept his feet only by leaning into the wind at an angle of forty-five degrees. Once he was used to it, the position was not un-comfortable. In fact, he sort of rested, leaning there.

The weather's plan of attack was obvious. Even Hels Helson figured it out as he waited.

"The vind blow oop so ve cannot make the drive doon, Ay tank," said Hels. "No drive doon, nosiree."

At once Hels Helson was seized with a splitting headache, the invariable result when he attempted thought. Johnny Inkslinger quickly ordered the Swede to repeat the Shanty Boys' Creed after him. The creed was a miraculous antidote to thought.

"My timber country!" chanted the timekeeper. "May she always be right, but right or wrong, my timber country!"

"May timber coontry," responded Hels dutifully. "May she alvays be right, but vat the hal, may timber coontry anyhoo, yesiree!"

He sighed happily, all thought subsiding and his headache magically departing. The chant and responses sounded on. Over in the shanties the jacks heard, and they scowled and sneered.

"What's the good of a creed?" they growled. "We

never think none, anyway. We never need no headache cure."

Hels Helson's one painful thought proved to be a true one. The weather was concentrating in a blow directly up the furtive course of the Big Skeery. It settled down into a terrific steady drive of wind. Great waves battered the Big Skeery's mouth. The stream, brimming with flood water, was flowing at its highest power, but, even so, it did not resist. Leaning easily against the wind, Paul Bunyan watched the flow slacken. The river was trying only feebly to course on. The waves mounted higher, leaping and snarling, thundering up in violent fury.

The river halted. For moments it hesitated, venturing timorously down its bed, then retreating, then shivering to and fro without flowing anywhere.

The shivers swiftly increased. Then, suddenly, the Big Skeery was foaming back upstream in a panicky flight.

Paul Bunyan swung desperately into action. He had planned to save the snow-heaped valley of the Little Fraid for a last defense, but the present emergency compelled him to fight with it now. Paul let the wind propel him up the main valley at full speed. He plucked dead trees as he pounded on and twisted them into a giant torch. Skidding to a halt at the confluence of the two rivers, he fired the torch and hurled it blazing into the dry ridge of brush hills atop the great snow bank.

Instantly the wind blew the fire into a white-hot inferno. The snow bank began to melt in an irresistible flood. Now, miraculously swollen to a thousand times its normal size, its underground hiding-places inundated, its valley foaming to both rims, the Little Fraid was as great a stream as its big brother.

Into the valley of the Big Skeery the torrents poured. The Little Fraid had entirely lost its identity, its self-control—every item of its being, in fact. It roared and foamed helplessly into the valley of the main stream, all its fears and hiding powers overwhelmed by the artificial force derived from the melting snow bank. The Little Fraid could not help surging on in the teeth of the battering blasts from Thunder Bay.

Crowding the near bank, cutting off enormous slices of earth, rock, and trees, the uncontrollable Little Fraid heaved on down the bed of the Big Skeery.

The main river was still beating a hasty retreat, rolling madly before the wind, on into the higher hills. Once more Paul Bunyan rested at ease in the wind, his stare fixed on the ridge of hills where the Big Skeery would have to make its last stand or go over. There the river must set its back to the wall, so to speak, and find a fighting heart. Would the river do it now?

It didn't look very likely to Paul Bunyan. He had been too rash, he mournfully decided, in feeding the Little Fraid so much snow all of a sudden. Had he held off until the wind was tired out, he might have melted the snow slowly and run the little river into the deserted bed of the big one for a log drive. That had been his original plan. But he had been too anxious to have the Big Skeery beat the weather and its bullying wind in battle.

All looked lost. Harder and harder the savage wind

pressed the frightened big river, driving it against the hills. In another minute the stream would be running over those hills, and that would be the river's end. Over the hills the Big Skeery would die into a lake. Now the river was mounting up them.

"Got a wrong notion this trip, I guess," admitted Paul Bunyan sadly. "A river like the Big Skeery just ain't got the heart. It won't turn like a worm will, after all."

He turned his eyes away, unable to watch the river take a licking that was bound to be the death of it and never fighting back. Paul Bunyan looked down the valley. Then he took in a sight that stiffened him up. Joy and pride shone in his eyes.

The Little Fraid, booming down the big river's bed, had found itself there. What it had found was a battling spirit and a fighting heart. Not only was the river charging on into the teeth of the wind, but it was cutting a big figure for itself. As Paul Bunyan stared, the little river cut not only one big figure, but all of them, from Figure 8 both ways, as it faunched and cavorted boldly down its big brother's bed.

"There's my kind of a river!" roared Paul Bunyan. "My kind, by the whistling old slingshot of David!"

Perhaps the Big Skeery heard and understood. Who can tell what rivers sense and know? At any rate, the big river began to act ashamed as the little one romped and battled against the wind. The Big Skeery slowed sullenly in its flight. An ominous mutter rose from its waters as the wind whipped them on for the hills. Then far down the valley the Little Fraid rolled round a big bend for a straight sweep into the waves of Thunder Bay, and the full force of the hurricane beat against its flow.

The flood waters of the Little Fraid heaved up in sheets of foam and clouds of spray. Ruin threatened the gallant little brother of the Big Skeery. It would not yield, it would not turn tail, but heaved and plunged in tremendous efforts to round the big bend. The waters of the stream were being torn into tatters.

A watery roar shook the hills. As it sounded, the Big Skeery towered in a twisting column of white fury, sank into coils, then struck back downstream like a thunderbolt, ripping through the wind, shattering it violently into so many harmless, gasping breezes.

In an instant the transformation was accomplished. The blind fear of the Big Skeery was changed into a blind fighting rage. Into the big bend it foamed and roared, shielding the Little Fraid, rampaging on for Thunder Bay. There its terrific torrents flattened the waves, and the aroused stream poured on, never slackening until it had emptied into Round River, Father of Waters. Thunder Bay, completely overwhelmed, was part of the riotous river now.

"A river *will* turn just like a worm will," affirmed Paul Bunyan joyfully. "The weather should have known better."

But the supreme test was yet to be made.

"Forward, Hels!" commanded the boss logger.

The test was actually a mere matter of form, as the river now ran. Hels Helson leaned over the Big Skeery as though he were going to dip a drink for Babe. It was precisely the same posture that had thrown the river into such a panic last autumn. Now the river boldly spouted a column of water at the Swede's Adam's apple. Paul Bunyan smiled to see the test succeed so well. But Hels Helson growled as he swabbed his drenched neck.

"A halva test," growled Hels. "Ay yust gat anudder vash Ay don' van'. Ay don' like rivers, nosiree!"

The jacks were already on the march. Not once did the river cringe or cower as the rollways were broken out and the logs boomed down. Not once did the river turn tail and run in reverse as the drive was made. Instead, it boiled and foamed so fiercely in every inch of its course that the jacks had only one name for the river when the drive was done.

"She's the Big Hellion from now on," they agreed. "That's the only name for a white-water river like this here one. And that raging branch there—well, we got to call it the Little Devil now. No other name for that fire-eater of a branch, no, sir!"

When the weather reorganized the scattered breezes and patched them up for another blow, the logs were all boomed. Paul Bunyan had made another spring drive. The weather raised waterspouts in Thunder Bay to wreck the booms, but they were easily nipped in the bud.

It was no trick whatever for Paul Bunyan to climb a waterspout and turn it off.

X

IRON MAN OF THE SAGINAW

DRY, hot winds blew through the summer and autumn. It was grand sleeping-weather for Shot Gunderson, the man of iron. Now he could rest without rusting. Through two dry seasons he slumbered, his slag beard resting on his boiler-plate chest, his cannon-ball eyes shielded by sheet-iron lids. The iron man of the Saginaw snored like a locomotive until an annihilating norther blew winter down. Then Shot sat up, sniffed the blasts, and shook himself. Not a squeak sounded. Not a spike of his hair had rusted. Every joint was oiled. Even each fingernail was like the blade of a new ax. The man of iron was in trim.

"Now it's me who'll do the finishin' job on that boss logger down there," rasped Shot Gunderson, as he watched Round River freeze a foot an hour. "I'll put the tucks in him and take the starch out. The weather won't need to bother."

But the annihilating norther blew on in its preliminary attack. The weather obviously did not propose to be cheated out of all the fruits of victory.

Down on Thunder Bay Paul Bunyan realized that he had to meet a double attack as he heard the first thunderous echo of the iron man's march and at the same time leaned against the first impact of the norther's attack.

"Got to ponder fast," decided Paul Bunyan. "Nothing but sagacity will do me any good here."

The boss logger of the North Woods wrapped himself in a shelter half made from thirteen mainsails supplied by the Royal Irish Navy. Covered to his knees, Paul Bunyan sat in his private padded hill and considered the situation through the night. By the rising thunder from the north he knew that the main attack might be expected at dawn. Then the norther would blast its hardest. Then the invulnerable and irresistible Shot Gunderson would charge.

Paul Bunyan soberly shook his head over the prospect of facing the iron man in a fair fray. He now knew that Shot was a human battleship, born to fight. Paul Bunyan, on the other hand, was born to get out the logs. For that alone would he stand up and give battle. In such an event he always fought fair. He was determined to stand up alone before Shot Gunderson now.

"Invulnerable," reflected Paul Bunyan. "That means nobody else alive can poke the iron man down. Irresistible. That means nobody else alive can stand up before the iron man's poke. But where there's sagacity, there's a way. I simply got to figure one out, like Joshuay did when he was up against the walls of Jericho."

Paul Bunyan said no more. He settled down in the

windy black shadows and turned the battle over to his
sagacity.

The norther blew down harder blasts with each passing hour. By midnight the advance attack of the weather
was raising the roof of every bunk shanty. The jacks
were roused from their blankets. Surly grumbles sounded
as they found themselves losing sleep. For every mishap
the men blamed their Big Feller. This was their oldest
custom in the North Woods, and Paul Bunyan bore
with it in patient fortitude. He had established winter
camp in a spot which seemed to be perfectly sheltered
from the northers of the freezing season. But if the
shelter failed, he would have to take the blame.

Certainly the shelter was failing now. The shanties
were huddled against the north bank of a huge wide
hollow in the bay shore. The first gusts of winter had
blown harmlessly over the shanties, and the jacks had
bragged of Paul's foresight. But this norther would not
be denied.

In its preliminary attack the norther hurled blasts
after the fashion of lightning strokes, driving in blue,
jagged streaks that raced through every nook and
cranny of the timberland. The norther raged over the
sheltering bank with the fury of a waterfall, then ballooned uproariously, catching the eaves of the shanty
roofs and raising every one. Peering through the swirling shadows, Paul Bunyan saw the shanties as a cook in
a great kitchen would see a host of kettles boiling, the
lids heaving and lifting from the pressure of steam. Just
so the shanty roofs appeared to the boss logger.

Under the roofs the jacks stewed about in helpless rage. Every man had five suits of red underwear, and he put them all on, with triple breeches, double mackinaws, and many mittens. It was useless to fire up the cambooses. As soon as logs were piled, the wind sucked them through the smoke-holes in the roofs.

"We got to get out to work," grumbled the jacks. "She's work or freeze in a norther like this here one."

But the stormy darkness was too heavy for labor. The only touches of light in the shadows outside were the clouds of snow blowing from the woods. Yells of panic sounded from the shanties. Paul Bunyan paused in his pondering long enough to order Big Ole, the blacksmith, to chain and bolt the logs to the cambooses. Soon each shanty had a rattling and clinking fire, the norther fishing through the smoke-holes in vain. The best the wind could do was to shake the bolts and chains. In a few minutes the jacks were swigging boiled tea in fair contentment. They began to notice what was going on, and they wondered what was making that rising beat of thunder in the ice of Round River up north there.

"The wind must have got under the ice and is blowin' it up," the shrewdest men surmised.

The others figured it was mighty likely now.

"That way it'll be rainin' icicles and frozen fish this time tomorrer night," the shrewd ones went on. "That's about the only trick the weather ain't pulled on the Big Feller yet."

Paul Bunyan listened grimly. He knew too well what the slowly and steadily increasing vibrations of that thunder truly portended. He pondered on.

One hour before dawn the fortunes of war brought another element into the famous fray that was drawing nigh. This element was the irrepressible mineral snoose, which found an active part for itself through the Big Swede. The latter was an important figure in Paul Bunyan's battle plan. But it was a new Hels Helson that faced the boss logger when the time came to make ready for the fight. The change was due to the fiery and explosive ore uncovered in the lone mountain of the old Saginaw.

Naturally Hels Helson turned to snoose for consolation and sustenance when the norther began to leap and bound into Babe's stable. The Blue Ox was untroubled. He simply got up, yawned and stretched, turned round three times, hoisted his muzzle, sniffed sleepily at the wind, lazily pawed the stable floor with his hind hoofs, and calmly curled up for more sleep, his chin resting on his hind legs, his eyelids closing drowsily.

Not so Hels, however. The norther had found a way down the back of his neck, and it twisted up and down the Big Swede's backbone in shivery curlicues. Hels had only one defense. Muttering savagely at the wind, he reached into his hip pocket for a barrel of condition powders. In his usual style of snoose-taking he held the barrel with his left hand, tapped the lid with his right index and middle finger, then uncovered the barrel and elevated a pinch the size of a bale of hay between two fingers and a thumb.

Instantly the norther changed tactics. The wind hurled a tremendous blast over Hels's shoulder and scooped the pinch of sizzling mineral out of his fingers.

It fell in a peppery cloud on the muzzle of the Blue Ox. Babe raised his head, twitched his ears, sneezed violently, and blinked reproachfully at Hels Helson. Then he curled up once more in his straw.

Ignoring Babe, Hels tried again. And again the norther successfully scooped and scattered an enormous pinch of the morbid mineral over Babe's muzzle. This time the neck hair of the Blue Ox bristled warningly. His lips curled, baring his teeth, and a muttering growl in his throat rose into a snarling moo as Hels Helson stubbornly grabbed for another pinch from his snoose barrel. For the third time Babe was showered with the stuff he abhorred above all else on earth. And for the third time Hels ignored all protests and warnings from the Blue Ox.

Babe shook himself, then grimly proceeded to squelch Hels Helson. With one lunge he seized the Big Swede's shirt-collar in his teeth and jerked the foreman backward. Without wasting a motion, Babe switched ends and sat uncompromisingly on the Big Swede. The wind was squeezed out of Hels with such violence that even the norther was blown aback. Babe settled himself on his haunches and sat with immovable stolidity. Under him Hels Helson was helplessly flattening into a huge human pancake.

Fortunately Paul Bunyan strode for the stable ere the dark hour before dawn had ended. The boss logger's sagacity had formed a battle plan. Hels was part of it. When Babe heard Paul coming, he silently slid off his victim, curled up, and pretended to be deep in a solid night of sleep.

Hels staggered to his feet. He was too dazed to realize that he was the Flat Swede now. And it was too dark for Paul to see that his foreman had the appearance of a blanket with human legs and arms.

"Come, Hels." The voice of Paul Bunyan sounded solemnly through the thick shadows. "You are to be outpost guard for the biggest fight the old Saginaw is ever to know. Forward, Hels, there."

The Big Swede instinctively obeyed. The wind had sunk to a steady breeze. This was certainly the last lull before the supreme storm of the annihilating norther. Hels wabbled in the breeze, but he did not blow down or off. He blindly followed Paul Bunyan over the ice of Thunder Bay.

A blacker shadow loomed in the thick darkness. This was the headland jutting into Round River.

"Here's your post," said Paul Bunyan, halting Hels in the lee of the headland. "You just stand guard till Shot Gunderson rams round the point. Then you grab hold on the tail of his mackinaw, if he's got a mackinaw. Anyway, grab his galluses or somewhere behind and hold on for grim death. There's the idea. The norther will be heaving its biggest blasts by that time. Your job is to slow Shot Gunderson down all you can. Then, when I come out to tackle him, you swing round so's he'll face the wind. That done, I'll fight him alone and fair. Understand, Hels?"

"You bat you," said the Big Swede mechanically. Only now was he realizing that something was wrong with himself. "Ay don' feel so gude," he complained.

"Nonsense. You're all wool and a mile wide," said

Paul Bunyan cheerily, little realizing how truly he spoke. "Take your post, Hels."

"Ay don' feel so gude, nosiree," worried Hels. "All vool and mile vide—bay yee, Ay tank that was yust the trouble—"

But Paul Bunyan was already beating back over the ice. The dawn had not yet begun to break. All he had seen of the foreman was a vague shadow, and all seemed well. Paul little dreamed that the flattening of Hels was the first flaw in his battle plan. The boss logger was all confidence as the thunder from Round River roared louder, as the spreading dawn gave the signal for the weather's supreme attack.

Dawn broke over Thunder Bay. In advance of the massed forces of the norther a barrage of heavy gusts drove waves of powdery snow over the ice and piled them in mountainous dry drifts on the shore. The lowering sky was menacing and bleak. There was no horizon. Cloudy sky and frozen bay blended in swirling gray shadows.

Behind the barrage of gusts and ahead of the massed forces of the weather Shot Gunderson thundered round the headland from Round River. He was only a vague, far-away form in the swirling murk when the shanty boys saw him. At first they thought this was Paul Bunyan. The Big Feller's private padded hill was empty. The jacks were awaiting the call to labor, standing forth boldly in the huge hollow of the bay shore. The lull which had ended the preliminary night attack of the norther had lasted through the entire hour before dawn. Always optimists, the jacks figured that the norther would blow no more. They leaned on their axes, waiting for Paul Bunyan.

The jacks should have remembered that a storm without a lull is no storm at all, and that the best weather-prophets agree in this saying: "The longer the lull, the bigger the storm."

This had been the longest storm lull known to weather history. The thunderous approach of the iron man of the Saginaw heralded its end.

The shanty boys saw the formidable figure in the dim distance heave round the headland. Suddenly it halted. Another huge shape had swung in behind the first one. Then the first and greater figure began to twist, clawing behind itself. The shanty boys were puzzled.

"What's goin' on there?" they asked one another. "That can't be our Big Feller. Nobody would have the gall to swing on to *his* mackinaw tail and play ring around Rosie with *him*. What's up, anyway?"

The norther answered them. Now the main masses of the annihilating wind surged round the headland and struck the two whirling huge figures. The first one jerked his arms up, teetered to keep his balance, then started as though hurled by a catapult on a direct line for the hollow where the jacks were congregated. Now the formidable figure was distinct. It bulked and heaved on at a tremendous rate. From its feet the snow parted in booming waves like spindrift tossed from the prow of a speeding battleship. Deafening detonations resounded from the ice. Behind the mighty foremost figure the second shape was a whirling blur. As it whirled, it emitted a sound like the buzz of a swarm of giant bees. The shanty boys were astounded and appalled.

"We're due fer a trompin'!" they yelled as one man. "He'll squash the life outer us, whoever he is! Let's scatter now!"

They were too late. Shot Gunderson was thundering down too fast. Even as they yelled, the jacks could see his spike hair and slag beard bristle. They could hear the furious clanking of his joints above the thunder of his stride. The iron man of the Saginaw was booming at the hosts of jacks with lightning speed. That whirling flat shape swinging from his mackinaw tail was the rig that propelled the iron man on.

"Stand fast," growled the boss choppers and peavey men. "We're due fer a smash-up. But never let the Big Feller say we smashed up a runnin'!"

Paul Bunyan's jacks proved their metal. The hard life of the Saginaw had tempered a tough shell around their old human nature. Not a shanty boy cowered. Every man jack made ready to die game.

"Good-by, old Saginaw," growled the shanty boys, and shut their eyes. "We done our best."

In the meantime Paul Bunyan was intrepidly preparing to carry out his plan for a fair fight. At the first glimpse of Shot Gunderson's approach he had crouched behind Babe's stable to await the outcome of his orders to Hels Helson. At first it appeared that Hels was to carry them out with unwonted brilliance. He dodged out of his hiding-place and seized the tail of the iron man's mackinaw without mishap. Not until the full force of the norther struck the two mighty figures did Paul Bunyan realize that his foreman was transformed. But when Hels began to whirl and whir, Paul Bunyan knew.

"Something has flattened him out," murmured the boss logger in astonishment. "Why, he's a regular propeller, Hels is!"

The style of Shot Gunderson's mackinaw made matters worse. The garment was more like an engine housing than anything else, and it had been a whim of the iron man's to carry out the style scheme further by rigging up a drive shaft for the mackinaw's tail. It was the shaft that Hels had grabbed and held in a stubborn grip. As he whirled and whirred, he naturally drove Shot Gunderson on like a battleship.

A glance into Babe's stable instantly told Paul what had happened. The Blue Ox was staring sheepishly at a wide depression in the Big Swede's bed. He responded furtively to Paul Bunyan's gaze and pretended to scratch trees from behind his right ear.

"You set on him," said Paul Bunyan accusingly.

Babe cringed and emitted a whimpering moo. But he was not to be punished at present. Paul Bunyan was already in action to save the situation. He charged in a gallop for the storeroom and seized three of his own axes. They were grand blades. When one was worn out, it could be worked into sevenscore axes fit for the regular choppers.

Swinging two axes in his left hand and hefting one with his right, Paul turned his gallop for the bay shore. He set himself against the norther, took aim, instinctively made allowance for windage, and pitched the first ax just as the shanty boys shut their eyes and gave up their last hope.

The shriek of the hurtling blade smothered all other sounds in the instant of its flight. The blade struck true, and a volcanic burst of sparks exploded from Gunderson's mackinaw tail. Ere the ear-splitting clang of the stroke had ended its first reverberations, the second and third axes were ripping crosswise through the wind. In a clanging riot of fire and smoke Shot Gunderson's mackinaw tail was severed, and Hels Helson sailed free. The iron man skidded to a stop, which burned the ice into slush for a hundred yards. Fearing wet feet, he floundered out of the slush, then leaned backward into the norther, and his cannon-ball eyes stared behind him.

There was something to watch indeed. Even the startled shanty boys stared only at Hels Helson. At first the Big Swede soared and flapped like a blown blanket; then he began to roll up and fall. But the norther speedily unrolled him, and now Hels soared crazily up and on like a giant kite. So he passed over the pine tops and was blown out of sight.

The jacks were threatened with a like fate as the bottom blasts of the rolling norther drove into their midst. The men wrapped their legs about scrub pines and their hands clutched others. The wind planed under them, arching their backs, but not a jack sailed away. The full force of the norther was high over their heads. There it heaved into the iron man of the Saginaw, holding him up.

Shot Gunderson blinked metallically at the soaring Swede until he heard a prodigious movement on his right flank. His gaze descended. Paul Bunyan, boss logger of the North Woods, was swaying at an angle for the iron man, boring into the teeth of the wind.

The iron man had his back to the wind. Paul Bunyan's battle plan called for an exactly opposite position, but he was forced to make the best of this one. At any rate, the shanty boys were safe. The logger still hoped to make the iron man face the wind. Just how to maneuver him into that position was the question.

To spar for time Paul engaged in a preliminary to actual battle. Shot Gunderson sneeringly participated. The iron man did not care. He had no fear or doubt about the outcome. He was invulnerable. He was likewise irresistible. Water was his only weakness, and he stood on seventeen feet of ice. So he scornfully followed the logger's lead.

"Go ahead and sashay," rasped the iron man. "But it ain't goin' to do yer a particle of good."

Paul Bunyan said nothing. Leaning hard into the wind, he grimly eyed Shot Gunderson, at the same time hefting a bay-shore bowlder in his left hand.

Suddenly he tossed it in the wind and instantly pulverized the stone with a blow of his right fist. Clouds of grit blew down the necks of the wind-heaved shanty boys on the shore. Grinning harshly, Shot Gunderson hauled fistfuls of black stuff from a mackinaw pocket and shoved them into his mouth. Then he struck sparks from his flint. A violent explosion rocked down the wind. The iron man of the Saginaw had fired a charge of blasting powder between his jaws without loosening a tooth. Paul Bunyan did not change expression.

His next move was to draw a sixteen-foot log from his hip pocket and set it on his shoulder.

"Dast you to knock the log off my shoulder here," Paul Bunyan growled.

Shot Gunderson responded by gouging a furrow five feet deep in the ice with the toe of his boot.

"Dast you to cross that line there," he rasped.

"I'm going to make you look human," growled Paul Bunyan then. "For that you got to be peeled. So here and now I start in to peel off your iron hide."

"I'm making a patchwork cushion outer you there," rasped the iron man. "To make that I got to take you to pieces first. So I'm startin' in to make pieces of you now."

That ended the ceremonies, which were to serve as a model forevermore when men of the woods engaged in battle. They failed to serve Paul Bunyan. The iron man had not budged from his position. He leaned back solidly into the norther, his anvil fists slowly but surely coming up for a fighting swing. The boss logger did not quail or retreat, though fully convinced by now that Shot Gunderson was actually invulnerable and irresistible. The rumors had not told the half of it about the iron man.

With a blow of his fist Paul Bunyan could smash bowlders into dust, and once he had even batted a falling meteor back into the sky. But he knew that his fist never owned the power to smash through the boiler-plate chest of Shot Gunderson. Nor could he hope to shake the jaws in which a roaring charge of blasting powder had failed to loosen a tooth. On the other hand, it was plain that a solid fist blow from Gunderson would dent the boss logger even as a solid sledge blow would dent the toughest wood. Too many such licks could not help but smash and splinter Paul Bunyan down.

But the boss logger had something that the iron man did not own. Shot Gunderson was fighting only for power and revenge. Paul Bunyan was fighting for the old Saginaw!

His logger's heart swelled with that mighty spirit. Here, he vowed, he would win for his timber country or else go down in his tracks. He would not falter. With the power of the Saginaw in his heart, he might not fail.

Now the norther began to prove that the biggest storms indeed have the longest lulls. After the lull before dawn the wind had steadily increased, first with its barrage of gusts, then with its first massed forces, and at last with a terrific flying wedge of wind aimed and hurled with solid violence at Thunder Bay. Now the weather unloosed its last and mightiest effort against the boss logger. The wind was backing up Shot Gunderson.

That was the iron man's main trouble when he tried to set himself for one straight finishing punch. The norther seemed bent on taking the fight out of his hands. It beat with incredible force at the iron man's back, trying to drive him into a charge. Shot hoped to finish the fight with one smash. So he drove his right elbow back against the wind. The norther could not know what he wanted, and it shook his elbow and wabbled his fist. Rasping out oaths at the wind, the iron man gripped his right fist in his left hand to steady it and to shove his elbow back into punching position. Slowly the norther yielded to the irresistible pressure, giving the iron man elbow room.

Rods away Paul Bunyan closed his palms together and pointed the joined fingers like a wedge at Shot Gunderson's neck. The bulk of the iron man broke the main force of the wind for the logger, yet it hit him hard enough to hold him off unless he wedged into it. Paul Bunyan did that now. There was not a second to lose. Gunderson was about ready to let his punch fly. And now, while the norther was at its worst, was the time for the Bunyan battle plan to be tried out.

Now Paul Bunyan wedged his hands, swiftly leaned forward with all his weight, and charged, all the power in his legs driving him on. His spikes held in the ice, the rods were reeled off in an instant under his plunging boots. At the end of his avalanche lunge the boss logger's wedged hands opened, then clamped like enormous swamp hooks around the neck of the invulnerable iron man.

Just an instant too late Shot Gunderson unloosed his irresistible fist. Paul Bunyan was already lunging inside the blow. The iron man's arm shot harmlessly by Paul Bunyan's dodging head like a log plunging over a waterfall. Nobody was there.

It was the boss logger's great chance. The force of his missed blow and the drive of the wind hurled the iron man off balance. He whirled dizzily. Paul Bunyan felt his own feet fly off the ice, but he sturdily kept his grip on the iron man's corrugated throat. Shot Gunderson drove his spikes into the ice and hauled up, still on his feet. Paul Bunyan made his cleanest landing since the time he tumbled from the high jump of bucking Big Auger River. His vaulting feet curved down in a royal arc and struck true. Now Paul Bunyan had his back to the wind. Shot Gunderson, white-hot with frustrated wrath, leaned into the wind to seize his adversary in a death grapple.

The boss logger was at last set to carry out the battle plan his sagacity had formed. The iron man was hooking him close. At his rear the norther was battering with increasingly furious blasts. Paul Bunyan leaned back carefully into the wind. He dropped his left hand from Gunderson's neck, leaving his own jaw exposed.

Then he roared tauntingly into the iron man's funneled ear: "Scared to try another punch, hey? Scared to fight and bound to wrastle? Where's your killer's punch, iron man?"

The taunt was shrewd. Certainly it was Paul Bunyan alone who had done all the wrestling so far, and it was Shot Gunderson alone who had tried to fire a punch. The iron man raged. He heard nothing but the taunt, and he saw nothing but the exposed left jaw of the boss logger.

"Show yer who's skeered!" he rasped. "Show yer who's a wrastlin'! Right now I shatter that jaw of your'n inter shavin's!"

Even as he rasped out the boast, the iron man dropped

his anvil of a fist down to his boot-top, to start an inside uppercut which would smash into the logger's un-guarded jaw. At that, Paul took a yet heavier lean back into the norther. He tensed every muscle. The iron man's irresistible fist started up like a huge rock heaved by a powder blast. In the very same instant of an instant Paul Bunyan yanked the iron man toward him with his right hand and pivoted himself out to the right like sheet lightning. The battering norther hammered by him, driving with full force into Shot Gunderson.

The iron man's fist was shooting up like seventeen cannon-balls in one. The norther hit the irresistible fist when it was only inches from its mark and deflected its course. Shot Gunderson himself took the blow. The in-side uppercut ended under his own chin with a shatter-ing impact, lifted him explosively, hurled him back-ward in an enormous arc—and then the bay earned its loud name as the iron man of the Saginaw drove head first through its ice with a crash that resounded in echoes for five hours.

Huge foaming waves and ponderous floes broke upon the boots of horseshoe iron that turned their calks toward the sky. The boots quivered once and were still. That quick Shot Gunderson gave up the ghost. Water was truly his weakness. He was as helpless as any battle-ship on the bottom of a bay.

As though appalled by this unpremeditated and as-tounding ending to its supreme effort against the boss logger of the North Woods, the norther expired at once into a mere gale. The shanty boys had held stoutly to the scrub pines throughout the fray, and now they thudded to the ground as one man. They sat up slowly, rubbing their eyes. All seemed like a tremendous dream.

But there were the boots of the iron man, bulging up from the raging bay. The echoes of the crash still rolled. And here came their Big Feller, smiling kindly through his beard, brushing his hands as calmly as though he'd had no more trouble than bread crumbs.

"All honor to Shot Gunderson," said Paul Bunyan solemnly. "He was the only man alive with a punch powerful enough to knock him into glory. Only the iron man could have licked himself. I want nobody but Shot Gunderson, iron man of the Saginaw, to have the honors of this here battle, by the old hallylooyer!"

The shanty boys cheered.

With Babe the Blue Ox hitched to the iron man's boots, Paul Bunyan hauled the famous fighter up the Round River ice to his home mountains. But that was not the end of Shot Gunderson. His real finish was as the richest iron mine ever discovered in the north country. History gives him full honors for the fight. Paul Bunyan never put in a claim for credit. His only part in the victory was to plan the battle so that the iron man would knock himself out of the Saginaw.

This famous fray ended the boss logger's war with the weather. The weather was not entirely baffled, of course, for to this day it remains the worst enemy of woodsmen. But it at least conducts its seasons in seemly order and for the most part keeps the peace.

Hels Helson recovered his normal bulging shape when he finally fell. Hels lit on one edge and the shock sprung him back into proper shape. He had learned his lesson well. Ever afterwards, when Hels hungered for snoose at night, he would always step outside Babe's stable to take it.

XI

THE BULLY BEES

PAUL BUNYAN ruled as the king jack of the Saginaw. From Thunder Bay he had logged a huge swath southwest to Round River and a greater swath back to the northeastern shore. The seasons had passed without another challenge to his authority. Paul Bunyan knew that Joe Le Mufraw still roved the untamed wilds of the Seven Mississippis and that Squatter John was making cornland below the southern bend of Round River. But these heroes had so far made no claim on the Saginaw timber country. Logging went on.

This summer, camp was set up in the hemlock land that circled the great Sauger Lake. On the dank shores of this dismal body of water the soggy hemlocks grew in such dense groves that the fiercest sunlight could not thrust through the boughs, and the trunks of the trees were black and steaming in the driest summer days. But it was different in the higher hills.

Up there the posy hemlocks bristled with thorns and crackled with dry bark and slivery sapwood as the summer brought them into blossom. For these hemlocks of the hills were truly named. They flowered in the summertime. Not in sweet-smelling, soft-petaled blooms, however. The posies of the hemlocks were hard. Every petal was as tough as a shaving of iron. The gritty pollen cut like sand when the wind blew it down. The posies of the hill hemlocks smelled harsher than the old blister rust, and they had the same dull hue. When the posies fell it was time to stand from under, for they dropped like mauls. The choppers who were not good at dodging had heads that resembled the nests of setting ducks, after a week of labor in the hemlock hills.

By this time Paul Bunyan knew that he faced the toughest siege of logging in all his Saginaw seasons. Here neither his muscle nor his sagacity could save the day. All depended on his men. Once the jacks gave up, logging would be lost. Nobody could kick on the weather. The rivers were right. The trees were the only trouble, and only the choppers and swampers could settle them.

After the first week nothing but growls and mutters rose from the shanties in the eventide hours. This was natural, as the jacks spent their spare time in plucking slivers and thorns from each other and in rubbing arnica on their heads. With every blow of an ax-blade the slivers flew from the brittle bark and wood of the hemlocks; with every third lick a posy would drop like a maul that had slipped the handle; and every time a tree came down, the thorny leaves leaped, darted, and hissed through the air like swarms of arrows. Six months of such chopping loomed ahead.

At first all the growls and mutters sounded against

the hard and thorny nature of the posy hemlocks. Then complaints began to rise against the Big Feller. The jacks remembered that King Pete had promised them the Year of the Good Old Times when he signed them up for the Saginaw.

"A year like that seems mighty likely," the shanty boys sneered. "We go from bad to worse follerin' the Big Feller up."

"How about goin' back to old Europe now?" ventured some of the weaker men.

"No we don't," the harder ones growled. "We stick right here and get out the logs till the Year of the Good Old Times shows up in the Saginaw."

There spoke men with hair on their chests and the old fight in their eyes. The jacks were proving themselves as true sons of the Saginaw. But Paul Bunyan doubtfully shook his head as he listened to the timber savages roar their vows.

"They got human nature in 'em," the boss logger solemnly reflected. "They simply can't help but have it, for they're men. Six months is a perilous time for human nature to stand such posies as these here hemlock ones bouncing around. Not to mention the stickers and thorns. I do wish," said Paul Bunyan fervently, "that something would happen around to salve their human nature up!"

As though in answer to the boss logger's prayer, a roar began to sound through the heat haze of the southern horizon. Paul Bunyan cupped a hand to his ear. The far-away roar subsided as the eventide darkened into night. But with the first glimmer of dawn the roar rolled up again. It sounded through the heart of the hemlock timberland.

All woodsmen know that there is no salve finer for inflamed human nature than honey. Let any gang of modern loggers be ready to go over the hump because of tough logging, and then let some rover of the gang find a honey tree, and trouble soon turns over. Human nature is sure to swell and heat up when the going is tough, but human nature can't help giving in and cooling down when there is wild honey for the hot cakes. So woodsmen are forever hunting honey trees.

The famous custom started with the coming of the two bully bees to Paul Bunyan's camp in the posy-hemlock country.

The bees belonged to Squatter John, and so their native home was in the corn and clover lands south of the Saginaw. The great squatter had gone too far with the bees, as he did with everything else. Greed was his main weakness, and it always made him overreach himself. With either corn, clover, or bees Squatter John would keep breeding up and up, until he would have a creation too big for even such a mighty man as himself to handle. Just so had the squatter's greed overcome him in the breeding of a pair of prize bull bees. He would not rest until he had two behemoths in his hive. When they achieved full growth the bees were so bully and tough that they scorned clover, and even fireweed, for honey-gathering. Finally they hacked the hive into splinters with their stingers and roared north in search of flowers hardy enough to match their lusty taste.

Squatter John followed the buzzaway bees in hot pursuit. On he pounded over valleys and hills, his chin whiskers parting in the wind, his cowhide boots kicking up the clay, a patched knee hitting his chin with every running stride. But at Round River the bully bees left their keeper behind. They roared on into the old Saginaw. At nightfall they paused for rest and sleep. At dawn they rose up roaring again. A breeze bore the rugged smells of the powerful posies from the hemlock hills.

"Here's what we're after," the bees seemed to buzz, as they roared jubilantly on. "Now we'll make us some honey that'll set our bee fur on fire!"

Squatter John had vowed that he would never stop until he had his prize bulls back again. So he swam Round River and followed the roar of the bees. But he did not cross the last hump of hemlock hills that rose to the south of the Bunyan camp. The great squatter was wily, secretive, slick, and sly. It was not in his nature to march squarely up to Paul Bunyan and ask for the return of his bees. In that event the boss logger would have freely given the prize bulls back to their owner and wished him well with his clover and corn. But Squatter John never dreamed that any hero could own kindness in his heart. So he lurked behind the southern hump, his auger eyes taking in all the mighty life revealed in the Sunday dawn, while he schemed to get his bees back.

Squatter John simply had to scheme about everything. He had more of human nature than any other hero.

Paul Bunyan experienced no astonishment as the two bully bees roared over the hills. Accustomed to queer and tremendous timber beasts and birds, Paul observed the manners and maneuvers of the bees only with curious interest.

As they reached the first of the posy hemlocks, the huge buzzing creatures swerved in their bee-line flight and flew in zigzagging circles over the rusty blooms and bristling leaves of the tough trees. At last they hovered, their heads together, as though debating their next move. The question was soon decided. The bees dived, each one settling on the harsh boughs of a hemlock, and prodding savagely into the posies.

For some time the bees attacked the powerful posies, slashing boughs with their stingers and ripping the hard hearts out of the blooms. So vicious was their attack that many of the posies fell, thudding into the dry earth like cannon-balls and raising balloons of dust. Ravaged posies wilted into harmless hollow cones as the bees buzzed on.

Now a triumphant hope swelled in Paul Bunyan's heart.

"I got to keep these bees," he thought. "They'll fix the posy problem there. All the choppers will need to do is follow the bees, and there won't be another busted head."

Certainly Paul Bunyan's sagacity was on the alert, yet he never dreamed that the bully bees were only beginning to make history in this Sunday dawn. But they soon showed the boss logger.

The bees were bulging in their middles at last, and

they soared heavily from the hemlocks.

"What could they have loaded up with?" mused Paul Bunyan. "I wonder, now."

Curiously he watched the bees as they buzzed sluggishly toward the camp. Now they hovered between the cookhouse and Babe's stable. Their heads together, the bees debated again. Soon they were pointing and nodding vigorously at Hels Helson's boots, which had been left out for a Saturday night airing. The boots yawned like great hollow trees just outside the stable door. Into the hollows dived the bees. In a moment they reappeared, flying light. They returned to the rusty posies of the hemlocks, then repeated their previous performance.

After seven visits from the bees the bottoms of Hels Helson's boots began to bulge as though feet were in them. Then the insteps began to swell. At this moment Hot Biscuit Slim strode from the cookhouse to see what all the buzzing was about. The cook was a shrewd observer, and the boots at once caught his gaze. From a crack in the leather of the left one a thick rusty liquid which simmered and crackled was oozing out. The alert cook's instinct of Hot Biscuit Slim caused him to insert a lean finger into the fiery ooze and then to wrap his lips around the dripping digit.

For a moment the cook stood transfixed; then he wheeled about and galloped for the kitchen. He reappeared instantly, with a smoking flapjack in one hand and a hammer and spigot in the other. Cream Puff Fatty, the second cook, wheezed and waddled behind him. Immersing the smoking cake in the simmering liquid, the cook passed it to his rotund helper. Cream Puff Fatty took one bite, then gulped the entire cake, and promptly fainted in a convulsion which unmistakably was an expression of ineffable delight.

The chief cook paid his helper no mind. Violently excited, he hammered the spigot into the crack, then galloped back to the kitchen.

"We got honey, men! Hemlock honey, by the old mackinaw!" The fervor of the cook's shout made even the griddle-greasers stop and stare. They stood gaping, the slabs of bacon strapped to their feet sizzling on the hot griddles. "A famous breakfast is to hand!" Slim shouted on. "I'm askin' volunteers fer a honey pitcher crew! Front and center here! Who'll volunteer to man the honey pitchers? Forward, charge! Hemlock honey on the flapjacks is to make the mightiest breakfast the old Saginaw has ever knowed!"

The cook's call was uproariously answered. Paul Bunyan smiled through his beard as he watched the volunteers gallop to and fro with honey pitchers, while Hot Biscuit Slim manned the spigot.

"Wild honey from the posies of the hemlock," reflected the boss logger, taking second thought. "So that's what it is. I wonder if hemlock honey ain't too wild for even my bully jacks. It's mighty apt to blister their gullets and scorch their craws. But if they are tough enough to stand it, there's the stuff to salve their human nature up, by the mighty old manna of the wilderness!"

As his sober second thought ended, another portentous event began to take place.

As the last honey pitcher was filled, Hels Helson came forth from Babe's stable. The formidable foreman yawned and stretched, primed himself with a scoop of snoose, then sleepily moved to pull on his boots. The left one had been fairly emptied by the cook, and in his drowsy condition Hels pulled it on without noting its hot and gummy innards. But when he rammed his right foot home, hemlock-honey gushers spouted and steamed up from all sides, spraying him to the eyes with sizzling and sticky drops. Hels stared stupidly at his soused leg until the bees roared down again.

Making another trip to what they thought were great hollow trees, the bully bees were astounded, and then outraged, to find a growling creature using the trees for boots, while their honey gatherings were despoiled. They buzzed violently around the Big Swede's head. Hels was aroused from his stupefaction. He did not like the looks or the sounds of the huge insects, and so he began to hoot at them.

"Go vay, har!" hooted Hels. "Who ask you to coom har, anyhoo, you fools, you!"

The bees were thoroughly incensed by that, and they began to fly rings around the Swede, attempting to attack him from the rear. He turned with them, still hooting angrily, moving faster and faster as the bees increased their speed. At last dizziness overcame Hels, and he sprawled, bottom up, over a hemlock hill.

The bully bees at once sat on the upturned bottom of Hels Helson and unsheathed their stingers. The result was hardly what they had expected. The snoose-hardened hide of the Big Swede could not be punctured by even the stingers of bully bees. The stingers tickled Hels, however, and soon he was laughing helplessly. At first the laugh of Hels Helson was like the gurgle of a brook; then his chuckles sounded like the rushing waters of a creek in flood; these ascended convulsively into the roar of river rapids; and finally his tumultuous bursts of haw-haws thundered like Niagara. In the cookhouse the jacks were shaken from the benches, and the honey pitchers were overturned. The camp was in an uproar.

Now Paul Bunyan moved to show the bees that they had to improve their manners if they wished to remain in the hemlock hills and make honey from the powerful posies there. Babe was fetched from the stable and backed up to the bees. Two switches of his tail brush sent the violent rioters tumbling end over end through the hemlocks. The bees got up growling. Their fur still bristled, their stingers flashed, and their eyes glittered in ferocious glares at Hels Helson.

"You too have got hair on your chests and the old fight in your eyes," said Paul Bunyan kindly to the bees. "I'll keep you here if you want to make hemlock honey. But even bees have got to behave theirselves in this here camp. Mind that, now."

The bees minded, and began to hunt real hollow trees for honey-gathering. The Sunday life of the camp went on. The jacks swaggered lustily, primed to the gills with the potent fumes and flavors of the bulliest flapjack honey ever heard of. Not a man talked of going back to Europe now. Not a jack complained about the Year of the Good Old Times holding off for so long.

"All we want is to fill up with hemlock honey and get out the logs," the shanty boys agreed.

It looked like a great logging season, after all. The trouble was that nobody counted on the wiles of Squatter John.

Paul Bunyan little dreamed that all this while two auger eyes were glittering over the southern hump. But there Squatter John watched and waited, scheming up tricks to get his bees back. He was a powerful figure. From amid the slashings towered the wrinkled legs of two cowhide boots like the gnarled trunks of old oaks. Jeans with patched knees bulged above the boot-tops. They swung from one gallus. Sparse chin whiskers waggled over the open collar of a hickory shirt. The great squatter's hooked nose was shaded by a ragged straw hat. There was a continuous trickle of hayseed from his scraggly hair.

Squatter John figured on, never thinking once to go on over and ask for his bees, and at last he had a sly scheme fixed up. He chawed on it for a spell, then turned his whisker over his left shoulder and let fly. The air sizzled for a mile. A mighty amber arc sparkled in the sunlight, rising like a waterspout, curving like a rainbow, then cascading down with a cloudburst splash. There was undeniable proof that Squatter John was the boss farmer of all time.

Still chawing on his scheme, the great squatter started back for his own country, without making his presence known to the king jack of the Saginaw. His scheme was all about a swarm of cow mosquitoes who infested one of his home swamps. Squatter John knew what would happen once these mosquitoes mingled with his bees.

"I'll get the bees back, shore," cogitated the squatter, as he headed home. "And I won't have to bargain with that sinful logger to get 'em back, nuther."

Such a notion would have greatly astonished Paul Bunyan. He knew nothing about it, however, as logging went on.

The going was still tough and hard in the hemlock hills. Under the sweltering sun the choppers and swampers stripped off their red undershirts every day, the better to stand the heat. Slivers from the brittle hemlocks still stuck them, flying from every ax-blow, and the darting thorn leaves kept them plucking one another through each evening. But the shanty boys no longer grumbled and complained. They followed the bees as they chopped in the woods. Falling posies bounced from their heads no more. And every so often a chopper brought down a hollow hemlock-honey tree. The men flourished on the flapjacks. They got out the logs.

Then on a blazing summer morning the scene of lusty but peaceful labor was changed into a spectacle of war in the woods. At first Paul Bunyan only realized that ax-blows were no longer ringing through the posy hemlocks. Then bellows of fright and wrath surged up to his ears. Paul Bunyan rose from his private padded hill and stared incredulously at the battle in the hills.

His gaze was first caught by six jacks who were down between stumps, held helpless in the scissors- and toehold grips of a vast mosquito who was attempting to jab a thirsty bill into their hides. Nineteen mates of the fallen choppers were charging to the rescue, swinging their axes as the bill darted down, but only deflecting it. Paul Bunyan's gaze swept swiftly on. There a second mosquito was already drawing blood, and the victim was saved only when two brave and cagy swampers thought to swing a crosscut saw over the mammoth's back and began to saw it in half. This mosquito had to turn all grips loose and fly, but it swooped back at once for a new attack.

The main host of jacks was flying for the shanties, and the main swarm of mammoth mosquitoes was swooping to bring the men down.

Paul Bunyan saw everything in one gigantic glance. Instantly he remembered how Babe had swished the bully bees from Hels Helson. Now he reached the Blue Ox in two strides. One twist and a turn, and Babe was backed against the woods.

"Swish 'em, Babe!" ordered Paul. "Show 'em what your tail was made for there!"

Babe obediently hoisted his tail brush, then instantly lowered it again. It was lucky for the Blue Ox that he had such a quick eye. For the two bully bees were coming down in a roaring rush, speeding like two great golden bullets, making the air smoke. Babe's tail had been raised in their path. The bully bees were roaring there for the swarm of cow mosquitoes. Their fur bristled at its best, red sparks shot from their eyes, and there was thunder in their wings. Babe's instinct instantly told him his tail could not stand against the bullet-like bees. As it dropped down to safety, some other instinct in the attacking mosquitoes swerved them into panicky flight before the bees. They stampeded to the north. Soon they were only a dark cloud on the horizon. Two dwindling specks speeded after the cloud, slowly closing the gap.

"They'll catch up, the bees will," said Paul Bunyan. But he looked puzzled. "I wonder why the sight of the mosquitoes stirred 'em up like that," he mused. "Could it be that the bees have got so fond of the shanty boys they'll fight for 'em? I wonder, now."

For weeks the boss logger wondered in vain. The bees did not return. Neither did the mosquitoes appear again. Squatter John could have eased the wonderment of Paul Bunyan, for he had cut round the hemlock hills in a wide circle and followed the roar of his prize bull bees. Just as the shrewd and knowing squatter had figured, he found them with the cow mosquitoes in a secluded lake land. He roped the bees, checked their stingers in his knapsack, and started back home. The bully bees had to follow or else lose their stingers forevermore. Squatter John had recovered his bees in his own sly and slick style. It was a style that left a powerful threat of trouble for Paul Bunyan, but the squatter was not the man to worry about anything like that.

Logging went on to summer's end in the hemlock hills. At this rate two more months should see the choppers hewing into the black and steamy timber of the swamp bottom. They were getting gaunt and stove up from their season of killing labor, but they kept on. The bully bees had finished all the perilous posies in the boughs. Many a hollow honey tree was found. The choppers swung on for more. This was truly the stuff to put more hair on their chests and more fight in their eyes. Every morning the sulphuric delicacy was swallowed down with flapjacks and fired the choppers up.

Everybody hoped that the bully bees would come back next summer. On a blazing day of early autumn the men thought their prayer was answered already. Down from the northern horizon sounded a roar such as the bully bees used to make. The jacks shaded their eyes and peered with hope. In a minute they were gaping at the sky, and then they blinked at one another. A whole cloud of bees seemed to be roaring over and down. Somehow a cloud looked like too many to the shanty boys. A presentiment of peril struck every man. Yet all stood at their trees. Nobody liked to run without a reason.

Paul Bunyan soon gave the jacks all the reasons they wanted. At the moment the roar sounded he was puzzling again about the bees following the mosquitoes with such fury and yet not stinging the invaders down. Now, as he made out the individuals in this cloud, he was puzzled no more. But he was considerably astonished.

"By all the morbid monsters of Reverlation!" Paul Bunyan roared. "If them bully bees didn't go and marry the cow mosquitoes off! And just look at the offspring that's come of it! Bills in front and stingers behind, and they'll get the jacks going and coming! Yay, Babe! H'ist your tail there! It's you who's got to save the day this here time, by the pious old lions of Daniel!"

This time indeed the Blue Ox was the sole instrument of salvation. His tail swept in ten-acre strokes above the jacks as they converged in a violent human stream which heaved on for the shelter of his hind quarters. The huge hybrids hovered impotently above. Under the stem of the guardian tail the jacks ran; then they moved in mass formation between Babe's hind legs; for half an hour the host proceeded under the shelter of his middle; and another half-hour's march brought them from between his forelegs, on under his dewlap and muzzle and into the shanty doors. Safely inside, the men barred the doors and blocked the smoke-holes.

The camp was in a state of siege as night descended. The mosquito bees persistently attacked the shanties and tried to cram in. Their attacks were dangerous indeed. A hybrid would insert a bill under one side of a shanty roof, clamp his stinger over the other side, start his wings going full speed, and thus raise the roof, while other hybrids reached in for shanty boys.

The jacks had to stand guard with axes and peaveys. Babe kept his tail swishing over the shanties, but his tail could not be in every place at once. It was up to Paul Bunyan to work out a way to raise the siege. So he reclined in his hill and pondered deeply through the night.

"I need to figure on the double nature of these here prodigious pests," reflected Paul Bunyan, as an idea rose up. "First off, they got mighty appetites. Nothing else alive is such a glutton as a mosquito is. There's the mosquito blood in these hybrids here." Paul Bunyan marked that item down, then thought on. "Now, take their bee blood. That gives them a mighty taste for all the honey of the earth. Let me cogitate on what it means to have bee blood and mosquito blood mixed, and I'll get an idea for putting perdition on them pests there, by the seven plagues of the old Egypt!"

At dawn the boss logger was translating a sagacious idea into action. First he pried Babe's stable off its skids; then he loaded the skids with a half-and-half mixture of hemlock honey and the heaviest of snoose ore. Next Babe was yoked and hitched, and Paul started him down the slopes to Sauger Lake. Seven miles down, the boss logger looked back. His beard shook with a chuckle of relief. The bee blood in the hybrids was urging them to follow the honied succulence that weighted the skids.

Paul goaded Babe into yet higher speed. The tantalized hybrids followed with increasing fury. Paul Bunyan did not let them catch up until the grim waters of Sauger Lake shone dully ahead.

Babe plowed into the scum, on into the deeps of the great old lake. The heavily laden skids were awash in his wake, but they floated on. The huge hybrids settled down at last on the heavy honied mass, succumbing completely to the blood of the bully bees and the blood of the cow mosquitoes mingling riotously in their veins, They glutted themselves so ravenously that they did not think of danger until it was too late.

In the center of Sauger Lake Paul ordered Babe to swish again. The hybrids were forced to take flight. Now indeed they knew their doom. Their bee blood had lured them here. Their mosquito blood had urged them into swelling their ten-gallon stomachs with leaden snoose ore baited with honey of the hemlock. One by one, the overweighted prodigious pests splashed, gurgled, and went down. The waters surged, and were still.

"Let that be a warning to all other pests," said Paul Bunyan solemnly, as he turned Babe for home. "Let them forever remember how bee blood can be their ruin."

All woodsmen know that mosquitoes took the warning to heart. Never since that disastrous day have they mated with bees.

XII
THE DISMAL SAUGER

IT WAS the dismalest of seasons for both man and beast in the old Saginaw. The wettest winter of history clouded down on the timber country. The weather was not making war again, as it brought the gray cloud packs on and made them pour; the weather simply seemed to have sunk into a spell of sorrow, grief, and woe; and it just went weeping through the woods the whole winter long. Amid the black hemlocks of the Sauger Lake bottoms Paul Bunyan and his jacks got the old life at its worst. They wished the dangerous times would come again, in place of the dismal ones.

Not a flake of white fell to lighten the somber woods. Never a frost crystal sparkled from a sunlit bough. The weather wept on, the clouds brooded low, the shaggy boughs dripped, ax-blades thudded dully in the soggy black bark, and the drenched choppers moaned with every swing.

This season was the toughest test yet faced by Paul Bunyan's men. As the wet winter dragged to a close, it was plain that the Year of the Good Old Times was still holding off. Again talk of going back to the old country growled up from the soaked shanties at night. But again the hardiest jacks roared it down. They were bound to stick to the Saginaw as long as logging went on, or until the promised year smiled down and called them to its glory around the Old Sawdust Pile. Day after day the jacks swabbed the rain from their necks, set their jaws, and grimly chopped timber.

Paul Bunyan as grimly held his men to the dank shores of the dismal lake. It was all or nothing of the Saginaw woods for him. His life was to log them off. The men here were the jacks for the job. Hair on their chest and the old fight in their eyes! That was the bully bond between Paul Bunyan and his shanty boys.

Their spirits held up through the weeping winter, but their flesh failed when the first feverish rains of spring steamed down. Even the Blue Ox panted weakly as he moaned through the mud, laboring the soggy logs to the lake landings. Hels Helson stood in a stupor of misery, his head sunk between hunched shoulders, hands huddled in his armpits, one leg drawn up under him. The gloomy rain fell on, now in huge steaming drops, now in freezing streams, then in a scalding downpour. After two dank weeks of such miserable weather the weakened jacks were smitten with hemlock fever.

Woodsmen know this affliction well. It smites its victim with both fever and chills. In a burning spell the blood rushes to the feet, and standing on the head is the only relief. But the chills are the more dangerous. When they grip a man, he feels a mad urge to work to get warm again. He cannot rest in blankets by a fire. Many a man has worked himself to death when seized with a hemlock-fever chill. This awful threat now faced Paul Bunyan's men.

The jacks were deaf to the Big Feller's commands when he ordered them out of the woods. Not until a burning started the blood boiling to their feet could he get them into the shanties. Then they roared in, to stand on their heads by the camboose fires. Paul Bunyan bolted all the doors. At nightfall woeful wails arose. The chills had come on again. Paul Bunyan's kind heart ached. But he could not unbolt the shanty doors. To let the jacks out again would be the death of them. They could never stand another spell of work like that last one, Paul Bunyan knew.

The great logger crouched in his hill by the lake shore and nodded in the rainy darkness. His heart was low tonight. His mighty game hardly seemed to be worth the candle, when his jacks were so full of woe. For the first time in his Saginaw life Paul Bunyan had a mind to send the men back home. He himself took little stock in the promise of the grand year. He figured that nothing but logging was ahead.

"Just logging," Paul wearily mused. "Nothing else for these here men of mine, by the old sins of Adam! I wonder should I let the lads go back." Darker and dismaler thoughts bore down on his mind. "I'd hate to see 'em go. I don't know why, but it somehow seems like we were kin. Yet I don't figure how we could be, the way they've got so much human nature there."

Still he went on worrying about the men, even more than about logging in the old Saginaw. As he crouched deeper and deeper, Paul Bunyan's thoughts softened more and more toward men. A stormy wind began to screech through the black hemlock boughs, but the logger did not know. Nor did he hear a mutter of thunder or see a wicked flare of lightning in the heavy sky above the swampy lake. The night was getting eerie now. A wild witchery of some kind was sinking out of the black sky and rising from the blacker timberland.

Crouching sorrowfully by the lake shore, the logger never dreamed that the greatest of northern timber beasts had at last howled into the Saginaw and had followed his logging trail. The timber-eating hodag was loping down from the slashed hemlock hills. He hungered for the fresh timber that yet fringed Sauger Lake. Paul Bunyan never heard the hodag's hunting howl, but it sounded to the bottom of the lake and brought the dismal sauger up.

The eeriness in the night and the witchery in the wind were a spirit made by the first bubbles and blows of the dismal sauger's rise. Every living, breathing thing in the hemlock land knew that the woefulest sights and sounds on earth were coming up. And all knew by the hodag's howl that the wildest and weirdest of sights and sounds were coming down. So the timberland night got eerie, wild, and witchwise, in and out and all over. The conks and all other little timber beasts moaned and sighed in their wet holes.

The great hodag loped hungrily on. Each lope carried him over thirteen stumps in the slashings, and his calked paws hit the dead earth with a solid sound. He was a mighty gray shadow against the lightning streaks. His shaggy tail streamed. He loped with his mouth open, and his saw teeth flashed, even in the deepest dark. And so did the great hodag's horns, for their prongs were like polished ax-bits. Ever and again the hodag howled and bayed.

As the hungry howls sounded nigh, the aged sauger prepared to sound his first battle croak. It was a fine fighting time for him. The wind was getting stormier every minute among the young trees. The mutter of thunder in the black sky broke into a crackling rumble, lightning ripped through all the clouds, and a roaring rush of rain threshed the waters of the swamps and the lakes. The sauger lifted his round head above the foaming water; he opened his wide, flapping mouth as though he was yawning, and a battle croak rolled from his belly, through his throat, and heaved the thunder back into the clouds; then he lifted his flat tail and fetched the lake a lick that cracked like lightning blasting through a hundred pines. But the croak sounded dismaler than thunder, and the noise of his tail on the water was mournfuler than the sound of striking lightning to hear.

Now the sauger made his first move to meet the hodag in battle. He waddled out to the soggy shore, where he sat up on his powerful tail and blinked into the stormy darkness of the hemlock woods. In a flicker of lightning the conks saw his front flipper feet wave. Then the shivering little timber beasts held their breaths and listened for the dismalest sound ever heard on earth.

Above the splash of rain and rush of wind in the tree leaves it sounded—that dismal drip-drip-drip of scummy swamp water from the sauger's cypress hair. The sauger croaked again, but the little timber beasts never heard his voice. There was only one sound for them, that dismal drip-drip-drip, which got dismaler and dismaler as the bulky sauger moved heavily through the wet, roaring trees.

The trees roared in the wind and rain, and up in the sky the thunder rumbled and growled; the trees groaned and shook around the little timber beasts, and rain blew and water oozed into their nests and holes; but what made them all so shivery and melancholy was the dismalest sound on the sad old earth. Drip-drip-drip. Drip-drip-drip. Soon the little timber beasts could hear nothing but the dripping of swamp water from the sauger's hair, and they were ready to die.

So the sauger moved on, profoundly plodding, savagely croaking, dismally dripping, toward two red balls of fire that glittered closely from the black hemlock woods. The hungry howl of the hodag was now unheard. Instead, a tremendous chomp-chomp-chomp sounded from the trees.

The great hodag was getting his first hearty feed of timber in months. All winter he had followed the slashings left in the wake of Paul Bunyan, where only bush and snags could be found for his meals. But at last the hodag had caught up with the logger. He settled down to have a feast in the rainy night.

But, hungry though he was, the great hodag stopped eating as soon as he heard that dismal drip-drip-drip sounding from the lake shore. Soon the light dimmed from the hodag's eyes; then a sad whimper rippled up in his long throat.

Drip-drip-drip on the moldy matted leaves and mushy sod of the timberland. The great hodag felt a shiver run up and down his knotty spine. He chewed half-heartedly on the soggy hemlock in his jaws and swallowed it heavily. He felt himself going under the spell of that dismal drip-drip-drip, just as the little timber beasts were going. It was a drepressing feeling which the hodag could not bear. He tried to howl it away.

This was the first dismal howl a hodag had ever made. It was never so dismal as the drip-drip-drip of scummy swamp water from the sauger's cypress hair, but it was sad and mournful enough to stop the sauger and make him grieve.

The great hodag howled on, and the grieving sauger dripped as he listened and stood. Finally the sauger lifted his round head, opened his floppy mouth, and began to croak out lamentations.

Then it was that the night got to be truly eerie and weird. "Ow-woo! Ow-woo!" howled the great hodag. "Gr-r-r-uck! Gr-r-r-uck!" croaked the sauger there. But louder and dismaler than all the howls and croaks was the drip-drip-drip of scummy swamp water from the sauger's cypress hair. The little timber beasts curled up in their holes. The great hodag felt himself going numb with the misery of it all. Just in time for him the weather parted the clouds with the first cold norther of the year. The moon shone on the dull water of the lake.

It also shone in the swimmy eyes of the sauger of the lake. Grieving tears poured out of them, but the sauger was plodding profoundly on again. He smacked his floppy lips to make the first bite.

The hodag's shaggy hair stiffened like the boughs of the hemlocks in the norther. He rose up in his fighting pride, reared back on his hind legs, then lunged for the sauger in a high and mighty spring. He came down on the sauger's round head. His saw teeth made shreds of the sauger's droopy ears in an instant, and with his ax-prong horns he smashed the great beast between the eyes. The sauger staggered, and then the hodag swung down and around and attacked him from behind. It appeared like a one-sided battle now, for the sauger was slow on his flipper feet, and he couldn't turn fast enough to use the bellows power of his leather lungs on the timber-eater. He did manage to knock the hodag down with a whack from his tail, but that only made the enemy go after the tail with his ax-prong horns.

It was a stubborn sauger, and he fought stubbornly on, despite the aches and stings in his hacked tail.

For two hours the battle lasted, and all the while there sounded the dismal drip-drip-drip from the sauger's hair. The little timber beasts shivered on in their holes, until at last the dismal drip suddenly ceased. The timber shook as a dull roar boomed up from its earth. Now all the little beasts rushed out to look.

The great hodag, feeling himself nearly overcome again by the dismalness of the sauger, had made one last desperate lunge, one final tremendous swing of his ax-prong horns, which shattered them into bits. But the sauger's tail went limp from the hard blow; he dropped thunderously to the lake shore and rolled with pain.

It was the hodag's grand chance. Up on the rolling sauger he leaped, and began to birl him with his calked paws. The sauger fought hard to stop his rolling then, but it was no use. The hodag was too good a birler for that. The sauger rolled like thunder for the lake, and the hodag raised a howl of triumph.

That was his last howl on earth, for the hodag made it as he jumped from the rolling sauger to the lake shore. The sauger had his mouth funnelwise as he struck water; he grunted, then inhaled with all the power of his bellows lungs and the might of his expanding chest; and the great hodag, weak from fighting and general dismalness, was caught in the violent suction and dragged into the lake.

A black cloud scudded overhead; then, in a flash of moonlight, the little timber beasts saw the lake all afoam. When the next cloud had passed over, the lake was still. And the night was still, too, except for the roar of the cold north wind.

It was nigh dawn before the sauger got his senses back. Then he discovered that the cold norther had been blowing into his open mouth all night. When he started to raise a croak of triumph over the lifeless body of the hodag, the croak turned into a cough so convulsive that it seemed his ribs would crack. The sauger felt a ripping pain in his right side, and he knew he was done for. A sauger had such a tremendous chest that when he caught a cold in it, he was as good as dead. Chest colds had ravaged the once mighty prehistoric tribe of swamp kings. And a chest cold did for the last and greatest of the saugers. He coughed his last in the first glow of sunrise.

"It must have been a dream here," said Paul Bunyan, as he shivered to his feet in the north wind. "A fearful fighting dream that bothered my sagacity all last night."

So deep had he been in sorrowful thoughts about his men that all the dismal and thunderous events of the night hours had indeed appeared and sounded like a wild winter dream to the boss logger. His thoughts were made up as he rose to his feet. He would give logging up and let the old Saginaw go. He had been too hard on his men and would send them back home.

"They keep a seeming more and more like kin to me," reflected Paul. "And even a logger ought to be kind to his kin, by the moldy old pottage of Esau!"

He turned to make a kind stump speech to his men. But the shanties were deserted. Looking on around, Paul saw the whole host of jacks moving out of the hemlock woods. They were arguing loudly, waving their hands back at acres and sections of ravaged trees, where the hodag had made his midnight meal.

"Thunderation!" growled Paul, his fighting temper rising. "Some other logger has been cutting into the Saginaw!"

He strode after the jacks to the lake shore. They were pointing now at the sun-reddened waters. All argument seemed to be ended. The talk was all one-sided now. The other side nodded in agreement.

"We ain't never goin' to leave the old Saginaw to be

the prey of timber beasts like that there hodag," the talkers said. "One and all we're going to stick with the Big Feller till he gets out the logs. What's the answer there?"

"We stick to the old timber country!" the whole host roared. "Loggin' goes on, by the old mackinaw!"

Paul Bunyan's heart swelled with mighty emotion, but he knew it would never do to show it to his jacks. They must never know that the Big Feller had gone soft on them here. So he took a ten-mile turn through the timber until he had his feelings hardened up. It was easy in the icy norther. Frost was already crackling in his beard. A crust was freezing on the swampy earth, and it would be good logging yet. The hemlock fever seemed entirely blown out. Paul decided to be hard about that when he got back to camp.

"How did you bust out of the shanties?" he roared. "Didn't I bolt 'em up so's you couldn't get out and work yourselves to death?"

The gaunt and stove-up boss choppers gave the Big Feller a tough grin. For once they had got the best of him.

"You forgot to choke up the smoke-holes," they growled. "And when the sauger went to croakin', he sucked us out. But we warn't in no danger of workin' ourselves to death then. The night was too blasted dismal for work," the boss choppers said.

XIII

THE COLOSSAL CORNSTALK

THE fate of the Saginaw was wrapped in a kernel of corn. Throughout the wet winter Squatter John plotted and planned to make the famous timberland over into the greatest corn country on earth. Ever since seeing the grand life of logging, his envy of Paul Bunyan had grown. Now the squatter was certain that he had a sly, slick scheme for land-grabbing in the Saginaw.

"Let ten cornstalks grow for every one pine," calculated the plotting squatter. "Ten to one like that, and the timber would be smothered out. Then that sinful logger would have to git, and I would take his outfit over for farmin'. Nobody can log cornstalks. They simply have to be farmed. It jest can't fail, this here new scheme of mine."

The wet winter and the hot and humid spring made the scheme look mighty good. Squatter John got powerful visions in his head.

"In three or mebbe two seasons I'll have the sinful logger squeezed out," mused and dreamed the squatter. "Then I'll beat the peaveys inter plowshares, the axes into fodder knives, the brush hooks inter huskin' tools, that blue critter inter a plow ox; and I'll beat the bunk shanties inter corn-cribs. In every pertickler, loggin'll go out and farmin'll come in."

Yet the great squatter was not entirely sure of himself. Ever and again his musings and dreams were broken by shivers of fear. It was not from dread of Paul Bunyan. Squatter John's fear was inspired by his own creation, the colossal kernel of seed corn. No matter how he prayed, schemed, plotted, planned, mused, and dreamed, the thought of the power and force that lay dormant in the great seed he had bred up made Squatter John shiver from bald spot to foot bottom.

For two seasons he had been saving the kernel, dreading to plant it in his own land. It was another example of the squatter's main weakness. He had bred too big in his greed for a kind of corn which should cram his cribs with the ears from a single stalk. Summer after summer Squatter John had concentrated pollen, and at last he pruned a prime stalk down to a single ear. One kernel absorbed all its mates on that ear and then swelled into such enormous growth that it smothered the parent stalk.

Now the colossal kernel swelled the sides of the biggest crib on the farm. The kernel lay flat, its ridges squeezing the crib roof. Pressed for pumpkin room, Squatter John had stored eleven hundred of the yellow globes of pie fruit between the ridges. Yet the valley was hardly half filled. No wonder the squatter regarded such a monster of a corn kernel with dread.

His dread was overcome, however, by the time the

one norther of the winter blew and froze Round River. Squatter John's greed would not be denied. It made him optimistic.

"Even if there ain't no holdin' the kernel once it sprouts, that won't be my look-out," argued Squatter John to himself. "I'll be on the safe side. For the kernel will be sproutin' in the Saginaw, and I'll be back across Round River and to home. I ain't got nothin' to be skeered about," he declared stoutly. "I don't need to worry a particle."

So he mused on, having grander and grander visions of cornstalks overrunning the Saginaw and smothering the pines.

When the ice was solid, Squatter John hitched his mule team to the great crib and crossed Round River. He left the crib standing in the Saginaw and took the mules back home. The squatter doubted his scheme no more as the norther blew on. He whetted his mattock and honed his shovel up. With the return of the hot and humid winds, he recrossed the Round and began to dig a pit which would hold the colossal kernel of seed corn.

Forty feet down Squatter John struck soil that worked and steamed like quicklime around the blade. It was strange soil to him, but he did not doubt its fertility. By its rich brown hue and its hair-raising smell he judged it to be rare soil for corn-growing. So he dug in perfect confidence, as the humid spring went on. The squatter was entirely obsessed by now with his lust for power.

"Loggin' goes out," he muttered with every mattock stroke and shovel swing. "Farmin' comes in."

At planting time all was ready. Squatter John feverishly rigged up block and tackle and rolled the colossal kernel from the crib into the huge pit. Feverishly he covered it with the steaming brown subsoil. But long before the hill was mounded, the earth around began to heave and roar. Squatter John's fever of greed instantly sank into a chill of dread. In his darkest doubts he had never imagined that the kernel would break into such sudden and tumultuous growth. But there was actually a cataclysm underground.

Dropping his tools in a panic, Squatter John made for Round River with a running jump. He struck the stream with his belly-buster dive; then from a heaving welter of spray his bony arms and legs whirled like windmills. Squatter John was heading home. He wanted no more of the old Saginaw.

For it was the subsoil of the Saginaw that had increased the potency of the colossal kernel a thousand-fold. That subsoil was nothing less than raw snoose ore. In any earth the potent kernel would have produced a prodigious stalk. Even in solid rock it would have grown grand corn. But in the feverishly fertile subsoil of snoose the kernel lost all control of itself.

In less than a day and night the corn mountain was raging into a corn volcano. The cornstalk did not simply grow; it erupted. The earth trembled, the timber around was shivered, and even the Father of Waters shook until it seemed to be a river of jelly.

In the center of the Saginaw Paul Bunyan heard, and he halted his westward march from Sauger Lake.

For a time he cupped his hand to his ears, listening four ways. Then he suddenly went down on all fours and held his ear to the ground. He got up solemnly.

"We've had war in the water, war in the air, war in the woods, and war on the ice," he said. "Now it looks like war in the bowels of the earth."

"Maybe it's just a hero coming up from China for a visit, Mr. Bunyan," hazarded Johnny Inkslinger optimistically. "That's how it sounds to me, like somebody coming up from China."

"You made a bad guess," declared Paul. "Just look at Babe."

The Blue Ox was sniffing the moist spring breeze that blew from the south. Then he began to lick his chops. This slender clew was enough to give the sagacity of Paul Bunyan an inkling of the truth.

"When Babe sniffs and licks like that there, it's green and growing stuff he smells," affirmed the boss logger. "Something big is growing down yonder to the south. It's the roar of its roots that shakes the bowels of the earth. That there's my guess. And it sounds like war to me. So here we go south to fight for the old Saginaw again. What do you say, Johnny Inkslinger?"

"My timber country, right or wrong!" cried the first and foremost patriot of the camp. "The Saginaw expects every jack to do his duty!"

The timekeeper's eyes shone as he heard the shanty boys cheer. For once they seemed to be responding to the creed. It did not occur to him that the lads were thinking they might get another shot now at the fine fishing they had enjoyed on the Big Onion seasons ago.

They were all sure that the Big Feller would never head south without a stop-over at the Old Sawdust Pile. The Saginaw was their timber country, but the shanty boys saw no sense in making a fuss about it. So they were thinking of fishing when they cheered the creed. The roaring underground threat of war did not trouble them.

"War is the Big Feller's look-out," growled the jacks. "All we want is a shot at a prime mess of fish."

But Johnny Inkslinger still deceived himself as the southward march was begun.

"Underneath their rough mackinaws and red undershirts beats hearts of gold, after all," he said to himself. "Right now every heart is throbbing to the creed."

The timekeeper said no more, for the pace forced him to save his breath. Babe was heading south in leaps and bounds. His back humped, his tail curled between his legs, his neck bowed down, his muzzle quivering in huge sniffs, Babe lunged madly on. Even Paul had to gallop to keep up with him. Hels Helson stumbled and fell after the first leap and bound, but the stubborn Swede would not unloose the halter rope. He held his grip, and Babe bounced him on. Every mile or so Hels hit the earth. He would light on his feet easily enough, as they were his heaviest parts, but before he could catch his balance to keep step with Babe, the halter rope would jerk taut, and Hels would be yanked up and over in a rainbow curve for another mile. Keeping the pace at Babe's head, Paul Bunyan did not notice the foreman's predicament until sunset reddened the Saginaw, and the home waters of the Big Onion shone and smelled from afar. Then he beheld Hels bouncing.

"Hang on, Hels!" Paul called cheerily. "Seven more bounces, and we'll be home. Just keep a hanging!"

Hels hung on. Johnny Inkslinger panted in his wake. In the rear the serpentine sled coursed over the hills with red-hot runners. The shanties swayed and heaved, and the jacks forgot all about fishing. They were limp in their bunks, their eyes rolling, their paws clasping their middles. This was the worst spasm of sled sickness they had known since the Round River crossing. Even when the big train jerked to a stop, the shanty boys kept to their bunks. The ceremony of leg-stretching was neglected.

It was sunrise on the Big Onion before the jacks tottered out, weak and shaking, haggard and forlorn.

But instantly every woebegone man stiffened and stood as though petrified, staring three ways; first at his feet, then at the second-growth trees in the old slashings, and lastly at the bed of Big Onion River.

Any one of the three views was enough to startle even the stoutest boss chopper into immobility. The whole host of shanty boys stood knee-deep in dust as dry as ashes. The young trees were withered and shrunk. The almost waterless bed of the Big Onion gaped with gruesome ragged cracks. Now hardly a trace of the stirring old smell of the stream was wafting in the burning breeze.

"Where are we here?" was the first dismal sigh from the shanty boys. "Where we been? Have we been sleepin' fer twenty year and jest woke up to ourselves?"

The spectacle of Johnny Inkslinger busily occupied

with figuring and measuring tools reassured the startled jacks.

"What's up?" they asked hoarsely, now noticing that their throats were as parched as the rivers and trees. "How do you account fer this here, Inkslinger?"

Johnny paid the jacks no heed. As he figured and measured, he talked to himself, however.

"No doubt about it," murmured the timekeeper, frowning. "Not a trace of moisture content. The country has gone dry."

"More of his creed stuff," sneered the bully boss choppers. "No blasted country can go dry."

Their weaker mates were miserably uncertain. They looked around for the Big Feller. He was not to be seen. Babe was also absent. Hels Helson was here, but he was in no condition to comfort anybody, even himself.

Hels was also parched inside. He could not work up a particle of moisture content with which to chew his condition powders. To Hels dry snoose was worse than no snoose at all. In his desperate attempts to produce the desired result his tongue had cleaved to the roof of his mouth. He jammed a crowbar under it and pried. But despite his mightiest efforts the Swede's tongue stayed stuck.

"It seems mighty likely the country has gone dry, after all," the toughest choppers admitted now. "Who would of believed it?"

Again the jacks looked at their feet. Every man yelled as he saw that he had sunk to his hips in the dust.

"Wade and swim fer the shanties!"

That was the yell from the quickest thinkers. It was a thought in time. The dust splashed and foamed as the men made for safety. By the time they were all back in the shanties the serpentine sled was riding a heaving dust sea.

"Maybe it's a hurricane blowing up from China," surmised puzzled Johnny Inkslinger.

Then a shout from the shanties made his eyes glisten with pride. Not a heart among the jacks had room for aught but prayers for the salvation of the old Saginaw. At last they were shouting the creed.

"Right or wrong, wet or dry, our timber country!"

From every pair of cracked lips issued those grand words.

In the meanwhile Paul Bunyan had charged on with Babe for the southern bend of Round River. So pressing had Paul felt the emergency to be that he had hardly paused after halting Babe on the Big Onion. The Blue Ox was as ardent to be on. He had stood quivering, sniffing deeply, and lavishly licking his chops as Paul Bunyan uncoupled the great skid chain and coiled it around the yoke.

"H'ist, Babe!" ordered the logger then. "Keep following your nose there!"

The Blue Ox leaped and bounded on with the first word. In his first jump his hoofs spurned the waters of the Big Onion, and three more lifted him to the valley's rim. Paul also started with a lunge, yet he had time for a glance at the river bed. He observed its rapidly sinking waters and was surer than ever of his guess.

"Green and growing stuff," affirmed the boss logger. "That's what it has to be. Babe sniffs it in the breeze, and his mouth waters for its taste. Its roots are so big they make the bowels of the earth roar, and they're so powerful they can suck the rivers dry. What could such mighty growing stuff be? Well, whatever it is, I'll stunt its growth, by the sinful old serpint and the pizen apple tree!"

The sunset faded in a grim gray haze. The moon rose like a face looking out from a shroud. Every mile the trembling of the earth violently increased. Deep roars resounded steadily from its heaving surface. Babe plunged steadily on, though he sank to the hocks in dust after every leap and bound. The boss logger guessed no longer. Now he knew.

It was no news whatever to Paul Bunyan when at dawn he saw what appeared to be a vast green cloud covering the southern half of the sky. It thundered in the wind, and its shadow swept steadily north, darkening the dry earth. Under the dark cloud towered a column of incredible size. It swelled visibly before Paul Bunyan's eyes as he charged on. Soon he was close enough for his vision to distinguish parts in the cloud, and he recognized leaves.

"Corn," declared Paul Bunyan, guessing no more. "It's a colossal cornstalk, that's what it is."

Obviously Babe was in agreement with Paul. He lunged on at such a blazing rate that the logger was left behind, and he did not slacken his charge and haul up until the stalk loomed directly before him. Panting furiously, his eyes bulging, Babe opened his jaws to seize

a giant leaf. But before he could snatch it, the leaf had
grown out of his reach. Babe tried again. The next leaf
fairly leaped from his eager muzzle. The Blue Ox
reared after it, in such a frenzy of eagerness that he
toppled backward on his hind quarters and ended in an
ungainly sprawl. He rolled over and heaved up with a
plaintive and pitiful moo of pleading for one of the
corn leaves. But they grew on before Babe could grab
them. Trying all his tricks in vain, Babe was moaning
with frustration when Paul pulled up.

The boss logger had too much to worry about to
bother with Babe's appetite now. The colossal cornstalk
appeared to be unquenchable and unconquerable. It
thickened and towered on, its roots thrusting ever deeper
into the soil and working like suction pumps. Moisture
content was drawn to the corn volcano in roaring subter-
ranean streams. Rivers were drained, lakes sank into
baking beds, springs subsided, the sap was drawn from
the trees, and even Round River was already only a
creek of its former majestic self.

"A lot of ruin already," muttered the boss logger
desperately. "I got to work fast to salvage something
from the wreck."

He waited no longer to heave into action. First he
unslung his three axes and threw the sharpest blade
into the cornstalk with the mightiest swing he had ever
made. The lick told. Paul swung back for a second one.
But even as he swung, the first gash he had cut grew
out of reach. It was plain that he could do no more than
chop notches in the cornstalk as it grew by leaps and
bounds. There was no chance to hew out an undercut

with enough depth for felling the colossus with the ax.

"Too tall and too fast, the cornstalk is," Paul Bunyan had to admit. "It certainly never can be slayed and slaughtered by nobody else alive. No, sir, nobody else—"

He paused in the admission. Now the sagacity of Paul Bunyan had its great moment. It threw itself into the breach spontaneously, full fledged, without demanding the beard-brushing and other coddling ceremonies which it usually required as sagacity's due. Not now. In this great moment the sagacity of Paul Bunyan gave all of itself without question or reservation, to save the grand old timber country from the supreme disaster of going dry. Now it found voice, roaring out in proud and defiant trumpet tones:

"Nobody else alive can slay and slaughter the cornstalk here, no, sir! But that's not saying it can't do a suicide job on itself!" the sagacity of Paul Bunyan roared.

The boss logger instantly began to suit the action to the roar. Snubbing one end of Babe's skid chain, Paul hitched the ox to the other end and started him at his highest speed around the colossal stalk. He followed Babe, urging the loyal creature on. At such a rate of speed the ox and the logger could traved in an hour the distance that a horse and man would need a week to make; so they were only three hours completing the circle. Then Paul Bunyan bolted the two ends of the skid chain together. Now he stood back with folded arms and patiently waited.

As the colossal cornstalk grew on, expanding

prodigiously even as it towered, the unbreakable skid chain tightened. Soon it was squeezing in. The chain disappeared in a deepening groove. Paul Bunyan smiled grimly in his beard. The cornstalk was choking itself to death. His sagacity had not failed.

Ere sunset the cloud of leaves overhead began to quiver as though smitten by a hurricane. Convulsive shudders raced up and down the stalk itself. The boss logger knew the signs. Just so pines quivered and shook before toppling from the chopper's ax.

Paul Bunyan called Babe and moved for safety. It was then that he stumbled over Squatter John's abandoned tools. The boss logger stared southward, a frightful scowl knitting his brows. He needed no more to tell him that the great squatter had slyly invaded the Saginaw from the south, even as the iron man had boldly invaded the land from the north.

"It's across Round River and to the south we're going to run to clear the choked cornstalk." Even Babe caught something of the grim significance of Paul Bunyan's tone. "Come on," was the next command. "H'ist south there, Babe!"

The two plunged on for safety and revenge. Round River was easily passed, and logger and ox charged into the country of the great squatter. Dusk was thickening about them when they roared into the barnyard. There they suddenly halted, listening.

A tornado thundering from the north was the first warning of the colossal cornstalk's fall. The immense and terrific displacement of atmosphere started tornadoes in all directions as the monster swept down; and then from all directions cyclonic thunderstorms were sucked back, to volley into the vacuum over the Saginaw. The earth sagged from the shock as the dismembered colossus struck, and spasmodic reverberations continued for nineteen hours. In all that time Paul Bunyan and Squatter John were the only beings who kept their feet.

The boss logger knew his man. After a violent pursuit over the shaking earth and amid the battering blasts he collared the great squatter and at once proceeded with the one certain way to punish and subdue him.

For Squatter John fist and boot were of no avail. He had no compunction whatever about taking kicks and blows. Nothing but mortgages would take the heart out of the great squatter and beat his spirit down. So Paul Bunyan slapped one mortgage after another on his adversary until Squatter John was groaning wretchedly under seventy-nine.

"I give up," he groaned. "I got enough. I'm your'n fer life, Mr. Bunyan. I was licked when you slapped the third mortgage on, but with seventy-nine mortgages on me I'm your'n till doomsday and forevermore."

Again peace reigned in the Saginaw. Most of the timber country had been salvaged from the dry wreck, but the Father of Waters was no more. The fall of the cornstalk had broken Round River's back. Like all dead rivers, the Round went the way of lakes. So Lakes Huron and Michigan were formed. The Big Auger shared the parent stream's doom and died into Lake Erie, making three additions in all to the Great Lakes chain. Now there were four. The fifth and greatest was yet to be made.

No longer was the old Saginaw a body of timberland entirely surrounded by running water. Henceforth the country was to be known famously as a peninsula. The body of the colossal cornstalk was its base. West of it the tornadoes had whirled the tassels, silks, and ears. The great squatter had not bred in vain. A mighty corn country was the fruit of his famous kernel, but it was not in the old Saginaw.

XIV
THE SAME OLD SAGINAW

THE promise of the Year of the Good Old Times looked like nothing but a royal lie to Paul Bunyan's shanty boys. They were having a summer of rest and peace, but they found no pleasure in it. All they could think about was that their good old timber country could never be the same again.

"Jest wreck and ruin," the jacks dolefully agreed. "We won't see nothin' else when the Big Feller takes us loggin' again." Then they growled sneers at the King of Europe. "Him and his promises! Look what's come of 'em here. Royal lies, all of 'em. Killin's too good fer a king like that there."

Paul Bunyan dared to hope. He had made summer camp in the old home valley of the Big Onion. The river had got going again in the thunderstorms and torrential rains that followed the cornstalk's fall. Paul hoped that other rivers had also recovered. The Saginaw might be a peninsula now, but certainly there were more logs to get out. The grand life he had invented must go on.

"We have just begun to fight," the boss logger declared to Hels Helson and Johnny Inkslinger. "Keep saying it there!"

Hels Helson was the most obedient of foremen. Every minute for three hours he repeated the watchword.

"We have yust begin to fight, you bat you!" roared Hels, shaking his right fist and gazing heavenward, as Paul Bunyan himself had done. "Yust begin to fight, yesiree!"

At last Hels unwittingly roared and posed before Babe the Blue Ox. Babe thought he was being challenged, and promptly charged. The Big Swede was hit so hard in the rear that his hip pockets were knocked over his shoulders and far into the woods. Hels hunted the pockets for a week, the watchword forgotten—and also the feeding of the Blue Ox. This neglect of Babe led to the first perilous event in the life of the newly made peninsula.

Paul Bunyan was too much occupied with preparations for a Fourther July celebration to notice what had occurred. On the eve of the anniversary of the entry of the Saginaw and the finding of Liberty Paul had a huge stack of scatter-cannon shells and a pyramid of cannonballs ready for his jacks to perform with on the morrow. He hoped with all his heart that the lads would find some fun and consolation out of a riproaring Fourther July. The preparations made, Paul retired to his oldest and easiest private padded hill for a fair night's rest.

In the meantime Hels Helson was returning with his

recovered hip pockets. He had discovered a bevy of bears using them for caves. The bears trailed him home, whimpering and moaning, sorrowful over losing such powerful-smelling abodes. In vain the Big Swede hooted and shooed them back.

"Go back to the voods, you fool bars, you!" hooted Hels. "You tank you keep may pockets foor caves all summer noo?"

But the bears stubbornly followed. At last Hels Helson paused to think what might be done about the bears. For three hours he stood scratching his head and thinking, with no other effect than that of a headache. Then Hels noticed that the bears were no longer about. Chuckling with relief, he tramped on for camp. Little did Hels Helson dream that the bears had crawled up his legs while he was trying to think and were even now snuggled in the depths of his hip pockets. Indeed, Hels did not discover their presence until the following year, when he took his regular spring bath. Then a turning inside out of his hip pockets revealed seventeen big bears and thirty-four cubs. Only a Hels Helson could have carried such a bevy of bears in his hip pockets without knowing he had them.

It was with a fine feeling of triumph that the Big Swede entered camp. A full moon shone along the Big Onion and smiled into his eyes. Hels Helson also smiled. Just once his mouth curved from ear to ear, and his cheeks shone until his face seemed to be a second moon. Then, suddenly, all was darkened.

The fearful stare of Hels Helson beheld Babe the

Blue Ox gobbling down the last of the scatter-cannon shells and the pyramid of cannon-balls!

"Oh, Ay gat it noo, Ay bat you!" moaned Hels. "Ay foorgat to feed Babe, and he gat hoongry—and he eat oop all the yacks' Fourther Yuly—and oh, bay yee, Ay don' feel so gude noo!"

The ruin of the Fourther July celebration was indeed the fault of Hels Helson. He knew well enough that Babe would eat anything but snoose, once his appetite was allowed to rage unappeased. He had neglected Babe, and now all the materials for the Fourther July celebration were devoured.

The anniversary was a day of mourning instead. Its dismal silence and gloomy quiet were broken only by growls and sneers at King Pete as a royal liar and by morbid predictions about the old Saginaw coming to an early end. Then the shanty boys began to brood about themselves.

" 'Pears like we're failures, after all," they brooded on. "We jest been blowin' bubbles all these here seasons when we thought we was loggin' so fine."

It was plain to Paul Bunyan that logging had to get going again. Rest and peace were no good for the jacks at this time. So he made ready for a cruise up the Lake Michigan side. By nightfall another perilous development had made it necessary to take Babe along.

All day Hels Helson had frantically fed the Blue Ox, to make up for his neglect of the week. It was the foreman's misfortune that the hay this season was half fireweed. Babe might have digested all the explosives in time had it not been for the fireweed in his hay. Every time Babe swallowed a bale, the blazing weeds touched off the powders in his innards. At last scatter-cannon shot began to zing and cannon-balls began to boom out of his jaws as he hiccuped and belched. The shot flew far, peppering the jacks. The unfortunate foreman stopped most of the balls, thus saving the walls of the shanties.

The shanty boys got miserably peevish as they settled down to picking the shot out of their hides. Paul Bunyan sorrowfully shook his head as he heard them muttering and mumbling there. Then a spurt of cannon-balls struck Hels Helson in the eye, and Dr. Johnny Inkslinger had to come on the run. He spent the whole night probing and prying with pikepole and crowbar under the Big Swede's eyelids, squinting earnestly through his specs as he searched for tormenting cannon-balls, while Hels hooted, groaned, and roared.

"It's west and north for us," said Paul to Babe at dawn. "Got to cruise out some tough logging for these bully timber savages of mine. Got to take you along till you're all fired out. Let's go find us a new pine river now! Yay, Babe! H'ist there!"

The shanty boys bucked up a mite as they watched the Big Feller and the ox trail out of Big Onion Valley.

"Never say die," the toughest choppers growled. "You can bet the Big Feller's got something up his sleeve besides his arm there."

Cruising west and north, Paul Bunyan traversed second-growth timber and slashings which marked the swaths of old logging seasons. Babe tramped at his side, belching shot and balls from the morning's feed of fire-weed hay. Paul Bunyan paid the explosions no mind. Only time could fix Babe up, and he left the cure to time. Every sense was on the alert for changes in the old Saginaw.

Squatter John's colossal cornstalk had left its mark far and wide. There was no longer any doubt about that. Paul Bunyan hardly knew the old timber country as he looked it over. The peninsula seemed to be little more than a shadow of the mighty old island. Each of the lakes that flanked the land was no more than a puddle in comparison with the Father of Waters, Round River, now, alas, forever gone.

"Puddle Michigan and Puddle Huron. That's what they ought to be called by rights," said Paul Bunyan grimly. Then his sense of justice triumphed. "But that'd hardly be fair, I figure, after all. Even if they can't hold a basin to the old Round, they're king jacks as lakes. Got to give 'em credit and a honest name."

The boss logger plodded dolefully on, tacking to the northwest. Here slick and shining rocks appeared, where even the top soil had been sucked down by the corn-stalk's roots. Ever and again Babe belched a cannon-ball at a rock, knocking it into flinders. Many of those flinders survive to this day, marking the trail of the Blue Ox along the Michigan shore.

The day waned, as Paul Bunyan had expected it to do. But it waned in a style that was new to him. Instead of mellowing out in deepening shades of gold, the sunlight darkened in smoky red hues. The forest shadows darkened ominously too, and at last utterly black boughs and leaves brushed the short ribs of the boss logger as he plodded on.

Certainly this was a timberland he had never touched before. Paul looked about himself and put his brain to work. Instantly he was figuring and cogitating with all the power of his sagacity.

It was high time. This was no regular pine country at all. Paul Bunyan's sagacity told him that at once. A shrewd glance at the setting sun, now a glowering red eye on a smoky and fiery horizon; a shrewder stare through the trees, their leaves coaly, their boughs and boles all black, snaky, and slick, the forest earth lying in smooth folds the color of tar; and, lastly, the shrewdest survey of himself and Babe—shrewdly and sagaciously taking in everything, Paul Bunyan knew that a powerful season of logging was ahead for himself and his crew.

Now Paul could even shut his eyes and be sure of that. Babe himself was getting the idea there. All of a sudden he let out such a mighty moo that he ridded his innards of all the remaining shot and cannon-balls in one blast. They soared toward the red and smoky sky in a black cloud, then showered to the earth. But that was not the last of them.

Instead of burying itself in the forest soil, every shot and each cannon-ball bounced. The whole cloud bounced sky-high. For an instant Paul Bunyan stared; then he nodded with certainty. There was experimental proof of the conclusion his sagacity had reached regarding this untrodden timberland. Now Paul Bunyan knew—but he had to act. The cloud was falling again.

"Yay, Babe!" he roared. "She's raining shot and cannon-balls, by the old Sodom and Gomorrer, and we got to get out from under!"

Even as he roared, Paul Bunyan leaped with Babe for their lives. It was not much of a leap for them, no more than a scant seventy-nine rods, and they lit without even springing their knees. But instantly they found themselves leaping again. As they struck the forest floor, giant hands seemed to reach out of it and hurl them on. Nine times Paul and Babe leaped without looking, for they had no chance to look as they leaped against their will. At the end of the ninth leap they began to bounce, and thus they proceeded for another mile. Eventually they bounced to a standstill on the shore of what appeared to be a rippling lake.

For once Paul Bunyan's heart was in his boots. His first move after stopping and getting his balance was to remedy that. For five minutes Paul stood on his head, shaking his boots in the air, until his heart was worked back into its proper place.

Again the boss logger stood up and surveyed the situation. Babe strolled to his side, stepping with more dainty care than one could hope to expect from such a bulky ox. But Babe had learned his lesson well. Already he feared and respected this queer earth under his hoofs. So the Blue Ox stepped daintily to Paul's side, rested his chin on a convenient shoulder, and stared and mooed at the gloomy sinking sun.

Paul Bunyan also stared at the glowering orb until it had vanished behind the horizon line. Darkening streaks striped the sky. The forest was an inky shadow

on the earth. Above it the black cloud of shot and
cannon-balls still bounced and soared, swooped and
hailed, as though a geyser were spouting them there.
Now Paul Bunyan was positive enough to openly declare his conclusion.

"She's the Big Rubber country, Babe," he murmured
through his beard. The murmur sent a breeze into
the near-by trees. Their boughs stretched. They seemed
to nod and yawn. "She's the last of the old Saginaw's
amazing and mighty timberlands. Here we'll have a
logging season as tough as any." The light of the old
times glistened in Paul Bunyan's eyes. The old roar
sounded even in his solemn murmur now. "Good logging is coming up. Wait'll my jacks feel this here
country bouncing 'em round. Wait'll I tackle log driving down that river there."

Babe responded with a solemn and sympathetic moo.
His bulging eyes rolled, following Paul Bunyan's gaze.
Here was a body of water which looked like a black
lake. But the sagacity of the boss logger told him this
was not a lake, but a river which was likely twenty miles
long and maybe ninety miles wide; there it lay, the last
of the strange and marvelous rivers of the original old
Saginaw, and the only one unlogged.

"The Big Rubber," Paul Bunyan murmured on.
"That is this here river's name. Will I drive logs down
it, now? I wonder. What if the last river of them all
should be the one to lick me and the jacks? That would
be the old life, right enough," he said, nodding sagely.
"To come through all this history a winner and then be
licked by a river, after all. Well, that's how it has

happened to heroes ever since old Samson lost his locks.

But Paul Bunyan could not falter or despair. He had too much kindness of heart for that. Soon he was thinking how much the Big Rubber country would mean to his jacks, and in his kindness the doubts and fears of facing facts were forgotten. Certainly Paul Bunyan was like no other hero.

"Come, Babe," he commanded. "We got to hustle back to the Big Onion now. There's good logging for the jacks, and we need to hustle with the news."

Daintily the Blue Ox wheeled about, and carefully the two great figures retraced their way. Then and there, as the last streak of smoky red faded from the sky, as the gloom of the black forest deepened, Paul Bunyan and Babe the Blue Ox invented the woodsman's stride. To this day every true man of the woods walks in a long, loose, knee-sprung, light-footed stride whenever he takes the trail. Paul Bunyan started the style for the purpose of walking without bouncing in the Big Rubber country. Woodsmen have used the stride ever since, mainly as a matter of habit and custom, but partly in honor of one of logging history's most celebrated seasons.

So Paul and Babe proceeded back to the Big Onion, without a bounce to mar their progress. The return was made in solemn silence, the boss logger thinking of his responsibilities as undisputed king jack of the Saginaw, and Babe, as always, respecting Paul's thoughts. The jacks were as silent in the home-coming hour.

In a simple stump speech the Big Feller described his

adventure and kindly asked for volunteers to log off the
pliant timberland of Big Rubber Valley. Every jack
responded with a roaring voice and hot shining eyes.

"Let's get out the logs!" The shout rose as though
one throat had made it. "We don't want nothin' else!"

"She'll be tough logging," warned the Big Feller.
"You'd never dream how that country can bounce you
up."

Then he smiled with fond confidence and pride.
Again the response was rising as though from a single
throat.

"We're glad she is tough loggin', Big Feller! That
proves she's still the same old Saginaw!"

X V

THE BIG RUBBER DRIVE

THE pines were black, slick, and slim. Paul Bunyan's choppers regarded the trees with approval as they spraddled, humped their backs, spit on their hands, and prepared to fell the first timber in the Big Rubber country. It looked as though the last logging job in the Saginaw mainland was to be a mighty fine one. The choppers and swampers easily moved over the pliant earth without bouncing. Only the Big Feller, Babe, Hels, and the timekeeper had to tread with care.

"Who said this here land would bounce us up?" grinned the jacks. "She's hard rubber. We ain't got the heft to make her give. So all she does is spring our knees a mite and make us feel like rubber heels. Here we go, men. Tough times is over."

They had all walked with the woodsman's stride while marching to their first morning's labor in the new woods, and all enjoyed the springy feeling in their legs and heels. It made them seem young again. So the jacks grinned heartily, and cheerfully set themselves for labor.

The earth and the timber were black, but the sun was peeping up, and its rays flashed from polished ax-blades sweeping back in the first powerful strokes. Nobody was gloomy. In shining silver crescents the blades whistled and curved for the slim, slick trunks of the dark pines.

Instantly amazing sights and sounds arose along the line of labor.

The usual resounding ring of edged steel cutting through bark and grain was unheard as the blades struck home. Depressing muffled thuds echoed instead. But the sights along the line were the strangest. No chips flew. Instead, every slim trunk yielded before the blade that struck it, stretched like a sidewise V, then snapped back furiously toward the chopper. Naturally the snap whipped the ax-blade out like a bullet. Every chopper was jerked off his feet and sent rolling. Everywhere in the woods men were tumbling in backward somersaults.

Paul Bunyan was ready with a remedy even before the jacks had scrambled dazedly to their feet. He had foreseen such an eventuality, realizing that the pines must partake of the nature of the land.

"Up and at 'em, men!" Paul roared encouragingly. "Dig in your calks so that you can pivot on the balls of your feet there! That's all you need to watch for. Instead of somersaulting when the pines snap at you, keep your balance and pivot on your toes. Just show 'em now what human swivels you can be! On your toes, men!"

Instantly the demoralized choppers were heartened and inspired. They scrambled up, brushed the rubber dust out of their beards, and set themselves for labor again. Now they were watchful and wary. Most of all they were on their toes. So another grand custom was formed. To this day woodsmen always make it a point to be on their toes when a particularly tough job is at hand.

After the first licks in the new style, grunts of delighted surprise began to rumble down the line. And no wonder. For now the slim, stretchy trees proved to be self-chopping pines! When a chopper kept on his toes and grimly gripped the ax-handle, the force of the back-snapping trunk did not heave him over, but it turned him on his toes. Thus he pivoted serenely as the ax-blade whipped round in a half circle. It struck the pine on the other side and was instantly snapped back again, while the chopper pivoted with it like the human swivel he was supposed to be.

Back and forth in a flashing half circle every ax-blade worked like a shuttle, driven by the bounces of the limber timber. Soon the pines were chopping themselves down everywhere in the black forest.

Then the mishaps began. When the limber timber fell, the trees did not shudder once and then lie still on the earth, after the fashion of ordinary pines. When these trees struck, they bounced enormously, most of them rising fully erect again. Where they had been severed, the trunks were smoking hot, the gummy sap oozing and bubbling up from the stumps. Thus a pine that bounced erect would stick to its stump and knit into a mended tree in a second. Many a chopper felled a single pine seven times, and still it stood. Paul Bunyan finally ordered the swampers to stand by to seize and mount each tree as it fell, so as to reduce the rebound.

The swampers bravely responded. Now for the first time swampers were heroes in the woods. All day the gangs mounted the pines, leaping on them as they fell, clinging like grim death to the slick limbs as the trees bounced and bucked under their weight. The swampers all got saddle-galled, but they did not mind. Never before had they held down their jobs half so well.

Logging went on through the winter with few more perplexities. It was a warm season with little snow. Now Paul Bunyan had good reason to thank fortune. In other regions such a season, without freezes to make iced roads, would have meant skidding in the mud. But in this country the pliant earth was also tough. It served as well for skidding as iced roads or snow trails. Babe abhorred bouncing and always walked with the daintiness of a toe dancer as he hauled log mountains. As Hels Helson always dragged his feet, the land was perfectly safe for him.

All the while Paul Bunyan was pondering the grim and dismal problem of pulling off a spring drive with Big Rubber River. As logging went on, his gaze never left the fork of the Big Rubber and the Little Gum. There the limber timber was piling up on the banking-grounds. Paul sagaciously foresaw the possibilities of failure. If he did fail, it would be for the first time in history.

"And this here's my last chance in the Saginaw

proper," reflected the boss logger. "What a mighty shame it would be to fail this trip. Well, by the smoky old bush of Moses, I just don't know the word. Fail, I mean. From now on I pass that there word by without even a nod."

Grimly Paul Bunyan made the vow. There was sorrow in the thought that his seasons in the Saginaw were coming to a close. Here was the last land to log in the Saginaw proper. On in the north lay the unlogged valleys of the Seven Mississippis. But his jacks did not have to go there. They had signed up only for the old Saginaw.

A testing time was coming for his men. Would they go on with their Big Feller? Paul Bunyan thought of the hair on their chests and the old fight in their eyes and believed the men would. No other life but logging could satisfy such bullies.

"But they got human nature in 'em," sighed the boss logger, remembering that evil which was born in men. "Why couldn't they be like they are, only having bear nature instead of the human kind?" he wondered sadly. "Their human nature makes men get such notions."

Paul Bunyan thought that because he heard talk of the Year of the Good Old Times grapevining through the bunk shanties again. The easy chopping and kind weather had banished all pessimism from camp.

"Wait'll the good old times come in the Saginaw and we get a chance to perform," said the jacks. "We'll paint the Old Sawdust Pile red. We'll make 'er blaze there!"

It was all a mystery to Paul Bunyan. For him there

could be no good old times but logging ones. But, then, he was not bothered with human nature. Heart, soul, and hide, he was a boss logger. He had kindness in his heart as well as hair on his chest and the old fight in his eyes. He would have to let the jacks go when the good old times smiled down.

"But maybe they won't," he hoped optimistically. "It ain't never sounded like nothing but a royal lie to me. Just a flimflam King Pete rigged up because he knowed it would appeal to the cussed streaks of human nature men have got in 'em there."

Paul Bunyan gave men up for the present, with a shrug of his shoulders that made the clouds dodge and scurry. He was grimly resolute about his own future.

"So long as my sagacity holds out, I'm logging on," he vowed. "I'm making a drive down the Big Rubber; then on and on I go, by the aching corns of the roving old tribes of Israel!"

With that, Paul Bunyan devoted all his sagacity to the problem at hand. Johnny Inkslinger had surveyed the main river, and now the famous figurer was ready with his report.

"The Big Rubber is a river ninety miles wide and twenty miles long," stated the timekeeper succinctly. "More detailed calculations indicate that in order to successfully drive these limber logs, Mr. Bunyan, you must have a river five feet wide and one hundred and nine miles, five thousand, two hundred, and seventy-five feet in length."

"Elucidate, Johnny," said Paul Bunyan, with ineffable patience. "But just kind of hold your figures down. You know how arithmetic can give me an earache when it's an overdose."

"There are five thousand, two hundred, and eighty feet in a mile," the great figurer continued earnestly. "Now I substract five feet from the present width of the river, which leaves the net amount needed for the suggested length. That is consequently eighty-nine miles, five thousand, two hundred, and seventy-five feet. This added to the present length of twenty miles gives a sum of one hundred and nine miles, five thousand, two hundred, and seventy-five feet. There's the arithmetic for it, Mr. Bunyan. I can make it look a lot handsomer with algebra," Johnny continued ecstatically, "not to mention geometry and pi. And wait'll you see how I've scaled the limber logs with elastic logarithms, Mr. Bunyan, just you wait now—"

"Stop, Johnny!" For all his kindness, Paul Bunyan simply had to interrupt at once. Johnny Inkslinger could be stopped in arithmetic, but never after he had once started talking algebra. "I've already got a couple stabs in my ear, Johnny," Paul said, in his kindest tone. "Much as I'd like to hearken to algebra, I simply can't risk my ear. I'll tell you, Johnny. You go and give Hels a lesson in the creed. He's getting slack on it."

Johnny Inkslinger fetched up two fingers in a happy salute. For all his passion for figures, the timekeeper never could resist a chance to give a lesson in the creed. Then he turned blissfully for the Big Swede, who was deep in the doldrums because spring was at hand, with a washing in store for him.

Paul Bunyan at once squared off at Big Rubber River.

The boss logger soon satisfied himself by experiment that the limber timber could not be driven down the Big Rubber unless the width and length of the stream were more than transposed. Casting one of the slick and slim black logs into the river, he watched it twist and curl up like a giant eel.

"Such logs need a river narrow enough to hold them straight between the banks, right enough," decided Paul Bunyan. "There's no two ways about it. I don't need arithmetic to tell me that. This here river has got to be stretched."

His next practical move was to manufacture an enormous set of water-tongs. In this invention Paul Bunyan made use of the tornado and vacuum principle, which he had observed and noted in the fall of the colossal cornstalk. Each tong was hollow, with spiral riflings in its bore, and instead of a point it had a suction cup. The idea was to attach the two cups to the lower end of the river. Babe the Blue Ox should then inhale through the hollow tongs; the wind sucked up the spiral hollows should have a tornado twist and pull; the river should then be siphoned into a solid grip and be ready to take its stretching.

To hold the head of the Big Rubber in place during the stretching process, Paul Bunyan laid a network of pipes charged with active snoose ore. Again the panacea proved its powers. It furiously froze the head of the river. There the Big Rubber was solidly ice-locked in an hour. The river's head was set for a long, strong pull.

In another sixty minutes Paul Bunyan was at the river's mouth with Babe the Blue Ox. The water-tongs were attached in perfect order and gripped the river relentlessly as siphon suction set in. The skid chain was hooked on, Babe was hitched, and the one-hundred-and-nine-mile-five-thousand-two-hundred-and-seventy-five-foot river stretch was started without a single ceremony. Not one gold key was pressed, not one silver tongue was unloosed to celebrate the greatest engineering feat of history.

On through the night Babe steadily plodded, bellying down as the river stretched near to the breaking-point and resisted the long pull. The river resisted in vain. The ice locks at its head were yet unbreakable. The tornado and vacuum principle of the water-tongs could not fail. All that counted now was the pulling powers of the Blue Ox. And he could pull anything that had two ends. The river-stretching job did not even fetch a grunt out of him.

At sunrise the rousing call to labor rolled up and shook the shanties:

"Down the river, men! We got to get out the logs!"

The jacks piled out in an instinctive response to the grand old call. Their woodsmen's souls triumphed over every other feeling when they saw the slender river that snaked by the banks of limber timber. There was a violent bristling of hair from every chest. Every eye shot fire from the old fight that blazed up now.

"Here's a drive to gab about ferever!" roared the

jacks. "Sharpen down calks and shine peaveys up! Down the river, you betcher!"

Breakfast was soon gobbled down. Files rasped from all the shanties. Grindstones creaked and whined. The ear-splitting uproar of steel and stone was music to the ears of Paul Bunyan.

"Maybe she is the last drive in the old Saginaw," he thought exultantly, "but she's going to be the biggest and best of all, by the muscle bulges of old Ahab! Down the river there!"

The last words boomed from his beard as the jacks heaved out of the shanties with their tools. Hels Helson took his post by the rollways. The logs flopped and snapped as his prodigious peavey pried them out, tangling into such knots that Hot Biscuit Slim, watching from the bank, then and there got his grand idea for the invention of pretzels. Paul Bunyan stroked his beard with a cheerful hand.

Valiantly the jacks untangled the knots, straightened the logs, and rolled them into proper shape. Soon it was a fine sight under the morning sun. Each limber log was held straight between the banks, for the timbers could not twist, curl about, or change ends in a river but five feet wide, and the jacks easily steered them on.

Down the snaky course of the Big Rubber the rivermen rode high and fine. The polished points and prongs of their peaveys flashed and sparkled in the sunlight. Soon the men were bouncing purposely as they worked the grand drive down river. When a jack leaped from one limber log to another, the timber he struck would yield under the impact of his boots, then spring back into shape and pitch the man up and on. Now hosts of rivermen were bouncing grandly all along the miles between the rollways and the first big bend. Their filed calks flashed in the sunlight, to match the glitter of peavey prongs. Wheezes and chuckles of pleasure sounded gustily from the river.

"Drivin' like this here ain't work," wheezed the bouncing jacks. "She's jest play, by the old mackinaw. Seems like the Year of the Good Old Times has already struck us here!"

"They can't get that out of their minds," murmured Paul Bunyan, gloomy forebodings again invading his thoughts. "I wonder if I didn't make the drive too easy for them, now."

Even as the boss logger murmured, his wonder was answered. All this while the powerful panacea had been freezing on at the river's head. It was dry ice at last, the coldest kind alive. As it froze into brittle powder, the ice began to give. Suddenly the river snapped free. Paul Bunyan's quick gaze saw it taking up the slack.

"Leap for your lives!" he roared.

He roared too late. Already the head of the released river was whipping up and snapping over like a giant lash. Ripples raced down its surface, increasing rapidly into huge waves as the river took up slack like lightning. The jacks would be swamped before they could take one jump.

All in the instant of an instant disaster threatened the last great drive of the old Saginaw. There was no time for thought, let alone action. The outcome was up to fate. And fate intervened.

Hels Helson and Babe the Blue Ox still stood by the rollways. The Big Swede stood as though thunderstruck, gaping at the head of the river as it twisted and slashed through the air. Babe began to bristle his hair and bare his teeth. But before one hair was erect or one tooth had glistened, the river had whipped its coils around his legs and jerked him sprawling.

The river did not know what it had done, of course; it was an accident of fate. Paul Bunyan acted to turn it to his advantage.

"Sic it, Babe!" he shouted. "Hold the river there!"

The Blue Ox needed no more urging. He no longer kicked and pawed in a panic for freedom. Even as the river uncoiled from his legs to whip on, Babe seized its frozen head in his jaws and rolled over.

At once a tremendous tug of war was on. Babe bellied down, all four legs stiff to the fore, his hoofs digging into the earth, his tail switching violently, while he savagely shook his head, held a solid bite on the river, and tried to back up.

Yet the Big Rubber yanked the Blue Ox on. The drive was still threatened. And once the river snapped loose and ripped free, it would be the last of the jacks. Even yet, Paul Bunyan saw in one desperate glance, they were not leaping for the shore. The limber logs were tossing and twisting under them as the river convulsively widened. The jacks bounced like popping corn. Yet they came down feet first, swinging peaveys to break log jams. Paul Bunyan's heart was nigh to bursting with pride as he lunged in to help the tugging Blue Ox.

He was just in time. The Big Rubber had jerked its head free, and this battered Babe with hard-water thuds. Paul Bunyan lunged to grip it down. But it was a slippery river, so the best he could do was to grab the Blue Ox by the neck and help him pull. Hels was at last charging in, however.

"Ay gat him down and Ay sit on his head har!" growled the Big Swede, hooking his hands and setting himself for a lunge.

Three times Hels Helson heaved his mighty frame at Big Rubber River. Twice he missed and hit the earth. The pliant land heaved him up again each time. The third time Hels struck in a sitting position. He was completely dazed by his terrific bouncings and did not know why he was sitting so solidly now.

The river knew, however. When Hels Helson lit the third time, it was on the still icy head of the Big Rubber. He froze to it instantly, and the river failed to bounce him high enough to shake him loose. Hels sat on. Babe held on, and so did Paul Bunyan. The Big Rubber quoiled down.

But it was still a battle with the drive. The river had taken up enough slack so that it now cut a wide swath as it bore the logs on, and its flow was in violent undulations. Every anxious glance Paul Bunyan cast downstream expected to see the limber timber knotting up in a jam. And it was doing just that in the heaving and surging flow. But the jacks were sticking to the job. When they were bounced to the banks, they instantly took to the logs again, their peaveys striking true, untangling the jamming logs, keeping them moving down the river. Tossed and battered, every man jack of the crew showed how mightily he belonged.

Johnny Inkslinger now fared forth to give the jacks proper inspiration. Figures were forgotten as the time-keeper bounced up and down the banks, shouting the creed.

"You've lived for the Saginaw, fellows!" shouted he. "Now prove you're ready to bounce till you die for your beloved timber country!"

The timekeeper carried a banner and also Paul Bunyan's old Quebec fish-horn. Every so often he lifted the horn to his lips and tooted martial notes. As the terrific timber fight went on, many a jack was left on the bank, completely bounced out, all befuddled with his bungs and bruises. Then Johnny had a chance to give cheery first aid. He was here, there, and everywhere, busy as a bee, bright as a butterfly, as gladsome as a robin. Paul Bunyan had a notion that Johnny was just being a nuisance, but he didn't have the heart to say so. Never had he been able to be hard with Johnny Ink-slinger.

Anyhow, the jacks were winning the timber fight. Two thirds of them were still clearing the jams as the sun darkened out. Nobody paused for meals or rest. The moon came up, and in its mellow light bouncing men still fought the limber logs with peavey point and prong. Not until dawn were the last valiants of the weary host sprawled on the banks, exhausted with leg fag, shaken innards, and bumped parts. The jacks were the color of the country now, black and blue all over.

But the timber fight was won. Johnny Inkslinger did

not need to wave his banner and toot his fish-horn to tell the men that. The Big Rubber had worn the stretch out of itself as Hels Helson sat on its head, and Paul and Babe pulled it to a finish in the tug of war. The river's elasticity was lost. With the dawn it was flowing slick and smooth again, holding the limber logs in place, taking the drive down without a jam.

Emitting growling moos of warning, Babe relinquished his bite. Hels Helson came out of his daze and got up hobbling. Sitting on the river's frozen head for a day and a night had left the Big Swede badly frostbitten. Paul himself was stiff and sore, and Babe had a toothache. Every jack bore dreadful marks of battle. Paul Bunyan turned to his men with an overflowing heart.

Never had the boss logger of the North Woods felt so strongly that men were his kin. In this the last drive of the Saginaw every jack had proved conclusively that he had hair on his chest and the old fight in his eyes. But there was something else. What it was the Big Feller could not figure out now. He only knew that it made his heart swell as he thought that nothing was too good for his men here, even if they did have human nature.

So he solemnly said: "Take the old Saginaw, men, if you want her. You've earnt her well, and she's yours. And I'm giving you the summer to make up your minds if you're going to take her or leave her here."

Saying that, Paul Bunyan stared broodingly northward. The Seven Mississippis waited for him there. By autumn he would be crossing to that timberland. He knew he was mighty likely to go without his men.

Bruised and bunged though they were, they were gabbing about the Year of the Good Old Times again. Somehow it made his heart sink.

"But what they do is up to them," said Paul Bunyan resolutely to himself. "Me, I've an urge in my ribs and a itch in my feet. Now and forevermore I have to get out the logs."

XVI

POKEMOUCHE THE RED BEAVER

PAUL BUNYAN did not know that the beavers of the Seven Mississippis had reformed into a new system of living which made them choppers of trees. This was because he remained in the Saginaw proper, where the life of beavers was unchanged. That is, they were water bears, living in river-bank caves and making their meals from careless fish and stray nuts and berries. But up north Pokemouche the Red Beaver had started a new life for his tribe. Under his leadership the beavers were getting out the logs for Joe Le Mufraw.

The mighty Pokemouche was the size of thrice thirty-seven seals; he was as red as a squirrel; he owned a tail so powerful and wide that he could splash all the water from a broad lake by taking the time and trouble for it; he had a kick which had tossed whales in the old Round River days; he could slash through a pine log with one nip of his tusks; and, to cap his qualities, Pokemouche the Red Beaver owned an omnivorous appetite for land bears.

The bears of the North Woods first took to tree-climbing to escape the appetite of Pokemouche; and the beavers of the Seven Mississippis first took to tree-felling in imitation of the bear-hunting strategy of their great red leader.

These were new habits for both beavers and bears. While the Father of Waters yet flowed, its one beaver, the incomparable Pokemouche, had been a fish-eater. He had never troubled timber then. Not until the Bunyan drives began to make their eternal rounds in the circular stream did the Red Beaver discover his prowess in slashing logs and felling trees. Pokemouche first tackled logs with the impression that they were a new kind of fish, such as the whales that had fattened him enormously in certain seasons. The fibers of the pines soon assured him that they were not fish flesh. Then Pokemouche used the logs simply for tusk-sharpening.

When Round River flowed no more, Pokemouche had migrated to the new Father of Waters, the Mississippi system. He followed its main stem until north of the Iron Mountains; and then he assumed command of the seven streams that swept on through a vast wilderness of layer pines to the west and emptied to the south in the vast wilderness of waters, Prairie Lake.

There were seven streams, because no one river, aside from the old Round, could have carried such a body of water. Nor could two, three, four, five, or six rivers handle this tremendous job. For even seven the task entailed considerable strain. More than once they had displayed a tendency to die into one lake. But as long as they lasted, the Seven Mississippis made a mighty water and woods domain for Pokemouche the Red Beaver.

His only trouble was with his diet. The Seven Mississippis were miserably deficient in fish. Only the catfish were large enough to be prey for Pokemouche, and he did not like their stickers in his gullet. So in a season he became as much of a land animal as a water one, roving the wooded valleys in search of savory meat.

Pokemouche found what he wanted in land bears. The kind, shaggy creatures, superior to men in their natures, in the judgment of Paul Bunyan, took to the trees to escape the Red Beaver. But he was too shrewd to be baffled. He had tried his tusks on logs. He knew what to do. With a nip and a tuck the Red Beaver could easily bring down a bear-filled tree. So he waxed fat as he ranged the great valleys.

Of all modern men only the Indians of the North Woods have a sympathetic understanding of beavers. Indians themselves have beaver blood, according to their history, and claim direct descent from the famous Pokemouche. However that may be, both beavers and Indians live in lodges, and in many other ways enjoy a community of understanding.

Pokemouche established a new order among the beaver tribe. Then he encountered Joe Le Mufraw. The river rover had just finished rough plans for starting up in business as a boss logger, in competition with Paul Bunyan. He had put in an order with King Pete for men who would serve as jacks. In the meanwhile he was waiting for the Year of the Good Old Times to shine down on the Saginaw. Then, so the river rover schemed, he would steal Babe the Blue Ox and Hels Helson from under the nose of the king jack of the Saginaw.

The Red Beaver changed the rough plans of Joe Le Mufraw, who saw at once that the reformed beavers of the Seven Mississippis would be better than men for jacks. So the Mufraw at once made advances to the great beaver, calling him "Pokemouche, my fine, good frien', *mojee de batan!*"

Woodsmen have never satisfactorily explained the eager submission of Pokemouche to the river rover. Certainly the Red Beaver owned none of the capacity for fidelity, loyalty, and devotion that the Blue Ox enjoyed. Nor did Joe Le Mufraw own the kindness of heart to inspire such emotions in man or beast.

The shrewdest guess yet made surmises that Pokemouche labored under a delusion in regard to his new master and friend. The delusion itself had two forms. In one Pokemouche apparently considered the Mufraw to be a prodigious animated tree. In the other the Red Beaver seemed to regard the river rover as a behemoth bear. So, just as modern Indians bow the knee in worship and awe before great gods who have the shape and aspect of the creatures the Indians hunt, thus did the Red Beaver submit eagerly to Joe Le Mufraw.

Truly the Mufraw looked like either one or the other—a pine of the seven valleys, or a black bear of the forests there. Of course he was immeasurably bigger than any bear or pine, but his size did no violence to the likenesses.

Joe Le Mufraw was enormously squat, shaggy, and wide. His feet and legs bulged like two mammoth black stumps sawed close to the ground. When the Mufraw faced the north, his shaggy frame seemed to spread from east to west, while his hairy paws dangled so far below his knees that his fingers were no more than eleven feet from the ground. Joe Le Mufraw was a man without a neck. His head merged with his shoulders like a black camel's hump. From a coaly mat of hair and a jet-hued jungle of beard his unblinking eyes stared like enormous knots. The river rover looked like a pine, slept like a log, and shook himself like boughs in a big wind when moss grew down his neck. But when he roved, then Joe Le Mufraw was the man who walked like a bear.

Though he was half pine and half bear in his nature, the Mufraw owned few of the instincts of the true logger, the conqueror of timber countries. Where Paul Bunyan had made a strategic start in the rich and kind Quebec country, never invading the mightiest and most perilous of timberlands until he was full blown in sagacity and experience, Joe Le Mufraw had made his start in the poorest and toughest logging on earth. The seven valleys were fine for river roving. For logging they were no good.

The layer pines of the valleys grew in groups of five. The foundation tree of each group grew in a horizontal position a few feet from the ground. Its under set of boughs had root systems instead of twigs and leaves, and these were anchored in the soil. Its upper set of boughs jutted vertically, uniting with a second tree. So a group of layer pines would continue to the top tree, which alone waved branches in the winds. A more awkward and cumbersome kind of pine could not be imagined. It was fit for nothing but bear-climbing and beaver-biting. Yet Joe Le Mufraw started his logging operations here without a second thought.

Certainly the river rover was a blundering boss logger. In secretly switching from men to beavers he was guilty of double dealing with the King of Europe. The royal gent would not resent this the less because he deserved it. More, Joe Le Mufraw had started logging in the land that loomed next for Paul Bunyan on the trail out of the Saginaw.

Wars were inevitable for Joe Le Mufraw. And he was no iron man. Instead, the Mufraw was a wooden sort of hero. It was no secret to either Paul Bunyan or the King that he could be split apart.

With the booming of the final Saginaw drive Paul Bunyan prepared to clean up and pull out.

"I'll hew to the trail," he decided, "let the men fall where they may."

But the men stayed with him for the summer and autumn job. The timber fight with the Big Rubber had bullied them up until they had no urge to loaf. So they joined with a will in putting the Saginaw into shape before the Big Feller had to move for next season's logging. Freedom was conveniently forgotten for the time being.

Paul's sagacity got going full blast on his summer's work. This was to put the Bunyan log drives in order and leave them in fine shape for the future. When Round River died into a team of great lakes, the drives had naturally quit wandering in an aimless circle. They gathered and piled on the northern nub of the new peninsula. Such a curious conglomeration of timber could hardly be imagined. But there it was, consisting of all the varieties of Saginaw pines, from the early onion ones to the limber timber floated up last spring.

"We got to sort it out, stack it up, smooth it down, and leave it all in proper shape," said Paul to Johnny and Hels. "What shape'll we leave it in? That there's the next question."

Hels Helson naturally thought a snoose-barrel shape reaching to the skies would be the best one. Paul himself favored a timber mountain as a shape the old Saginaw would like.

"The country's got none too many mountains, anyhow," he said. "Give her the Old Sawdust Pile on the Big Onion and Timber Mountain on the northern nub here, and I bet the Saginaw'll be proud."

But Johnny Inkslinger insisted on a bridge.

"I've never done nothing famous yet, Mr. Bunyan," said the timekeeper plaintively. "Why not let me build a bridge here? There's nothing like a bridge to work figures on. I could use all I got, from simple sums to pi."

The boss logger reflected. His sagacity saw possibilities in a bridge which were never dreamed of by Johnny Inkslinger. So he gave the timekeeper the nod.

In a week Bunyan Bridge was started. The jacks went to it with a will, swarming the miles of tangled logs from dawn to dusk each day, following with their peaveys the figures unloosed by Johnny Inkslinger in a steady stream.

At first the men made hardly a murmur about the

Year of the Good Old Times. They seemed to have forgotten their new freedom. Every stranded old drive they tackled reminded them of some mighty logging time in the Saginaw. Throughout the summer each night was loud with talk about past logging seasons.

But as autumn deepened, the talk changed. Bunyan Bridge was taking shape. Johnny Inkslinger only had to put on the finishing touches and curlicues with the limber timber. The jacks remembered that they were men. Soon their Big Feller was hearing such feverish notions as this from the bunk shanties at eventide:

"How do we *know* we got to wait till New Year's? Does a year *have* to start jest on that there day? Who said so, anyhow? Is they a *law* on it? Not much! Now looky here. Mebbe the Year of the Good Old Times is goin' to have *fifteen months* in it, and hence and so forth is already started this very minnit and now! Men, give 'er a thought there!"

Then Paul Bunyan all but gave up hope. It certainly looked as though he would need new jacks if he was to log on. So he sent his first message in years to his old employment agent.

"How about some more men with hair on their chests and the old fight in their eyes for a new logging job?" the message simply said.

In time the carrier eagle returned with a note written by Pete Barnum in his capacity as King of Europe. In it he evaded the issue, following the oldest custom of kings.

"What's all the work about?" the royal gent wanted to know. "I'm kind of curious to know before I send more men. What's your big aim in getting out the logs there?"

The answer was easy for Paul Bunyan, Real American.

"What is my big aim in logging, Your Nibs wants to know," he wrote back. "Come to think about it, King, I aim to please. That's all. I just strive to please, by the sweet old psalms of David! Now, how about some more men?"

There was no reply. The long silence was profoundly portentous to Paul Bunyan. His sagacity told him that King Pete had something up his sleeve besides the royal elbow. Pondering in his private padded hill, the boss logger surmised that unseen powers were moving to crowd over him. Yet he did not know which way to turn. He needed jacks to go on with logging. But more and more the Saginaw veterans were gabbing of the time to come around the Old Sawdust Pile. Winter was nigh. A move must soon be made.

Peering through the star gleams and shadows to the north, Paul Bunyan vainly tried to read his future there.

"Such a powerful lot of stars," he mused philosophically. "So pesky little light."

But with autumn his future was stirring to unfold in the first valley of the Seven Mississippis. When the frosts began to snap, Pokemouche lined up his tribe, and chopping started.

And now another mighty force began to shake the war clouds up.

In the plain that lay between the Iron Mountains and the junction of Lakes Huron and Michigan, Babe the

Blue Ox, in care of Hels Helson, was pasturing through the autumn boom grass. Steadily northward they browsed through the booming blades. Paul Bunyan had never suspected danger in the rich pasturage there.

But war clouds were bound to thicken. The Red Beaver and the Blue Ox were natural enemies and rivals now.

Joe Le Mufraw enjoyed one logging day. It was a stirring morning for chopping when the start was made. Cold gray fog massed before the dawn. The Mufraw's soughing breath sent another fog rolling over the forests of layer pines as the beavers were called out.

The newly fledged beaver jacks emerged obediently from their lodges, Pokemouche leading them on. They did not move steadily to labor, but paused every so often to sniff and blink. Yet they did not halt to gab and argue, as men would have done, and so the beavers made good time on their way to the woods. Pokemouche himself often paused for sniffs and blinks, but these were at Joe Le Mufraw.

The Red Beaver never could make up his mind about his master and friend. Now when he blinked, he saw a prodigious pine with black shaggy boughs. Then as he sniffed, he smelled a bear. It was a puzzle which forever tantalized Pokemouche, but he did no more than sniff and blink about it. He never stopped work to rack his poor head with the puzzle, as a man would have done.

Logging went on. Throughout the forest the beaver tusks rang with a music so unbroken as to be monotonous.

The chips flew fine and fast. Every cut was as slick and clean as though surfaced by a plane. The layer pines crashed in a steady thunder. With only slight pauses for sniffing and blinking, each crew of incomparable choppers separated every pine group into five logs, trimmed the logs clean, paused but once, then paddled on for more ardent labor.

Pokemouche was swung round for skidding by Joe Le Mufraw. The Red Beaver, unlike the Blue Ox, needed no yoke or skid chain. His tail was enough. Into its great open spaces the river rover rolled the logs. Soon the first bank of timber was rising beside the first river of the Seven Mississippis. The Red Beaver skidded with a contented heart. To him were given the bears that fell with the trees.

So the first day of the new logging operation went on as busily as the first day of honey-gathering in a beehive. Joe Le Mufraw's heart was nigh to splintering with pride. He had never dreamed that beavers would be half so good as choppers. Ambition gripped the river rover like a choker rope. Tomorrow, he thought, he would rove to the other six valleys and put the beavers there to work at once. Then he could log all seven valleys this season as easily as the one he had planned for. With this job finished, he could log on west long before Paul Bunyan had quit the Saginaw.

So Joe Le Mufraw ambitiously schemed. It never occurred to him that the king jack of the Saginaw would ever leave that country without his men. The river rover was utterly possessed by his relentless ambition as darkness closed over the valleys. He ordered the beavers to their lodges. All his shagginess shook with pleasure over the way things were going, and he soughed with pride and hope. Of a certainty beavers were better than men in the woods. They rustled their own grub. Beavers did not demand blankets. Joe Le Mufraw wished he had started logging long ago.

He forgot how much he owed to Pokemouche.

But with the next nightfall Joe Le Mufraw was remembering. The beavers of the other six valleys had refused to lift a tusk for him without working-orders from Pokemouche. His pride deflated, the river rover stumped heavily for home.

Tomorrow, he thought, he would take the Red Beaver along on his cruising trip, and then the unreformed little beavers would have to go to work. Yet Joe Le Mufraw worried. Now he knew how much he owed to Pokemouche. It was too much. Pokemouche might get too proud and in the end try to boss his master and friend.

His logging no longer looked so promising to the river rover. But the worst was to come.

As Joe Le Mufraw stumped into the first of the seven valleys, his ears were smitten by an uproar of battle. Smashing through the trees, his enormous knots of eyes got blacker with fear as they saw Paul Bunyan's Blue Ox and his own Red Beaver heaving mountainously into battle. Seven avalanches seemed to be rolling as the thunder of the fight shuddered seven ways.

XVII

THE SEVEN MISSISSIPPIS

NEVER dreaming that a Reformed Order of Beavers had been started in the lodges of the north by Pokemouche, Paul Bunyan had considered only one danger when Hels Helson took Babe north for browsing. So the boss logger had issued only one warning.

"Go ahead and fatten Babe up," was Paul's simple command. Then the warning sounded. "Just don't venture into the Seven Mississippis, though. I have a notion those rivers can't stand the strain much longer. They're apt to die into a great lake any time. That would make a pile of standing water. You and Babe can't risk being caught in the middle of it."

"You bat you," Hels Helson heartily agreed. "Ay vould gat vash, and Ay vas vash plenty in the Saginaw har, yesiree."

Pasturing had peacefully proceeded until the Blue Ox browsed nigh the forbidden valleys. There, as an autumn eventide clouded down, the Big Swede dutifully struggled to change his thoughts of snoose to thoughts of home.

It was a hard task for Hels. As the twilight shadows thickened, he yearned powerfully for a fresh supply of his condition powders. There were seventeen barrels in his hip pockets, but the contents had begun to dry out in the days of browsing. Dry snoose was as dangerous as it was flavorless. Without its natural moisture content, the panacea was highly explosive. To conserve his main necessity Hels Helson had to be seated with care while he watched Babe pasture here.

But at last the formidable foreman got his mind back on his duty. The long halter rope was tightening. A mile or more to the north Babe was nudging over the rim of the first perilous valley. Guarding his hip pockets, Hels got up to go. He turned toward the homeward trail, taking a firm grip on the leading rope. Hels drew in a stout breath. Frost was snapping fiercely in the eventide air. This was chopping-weather. Tomorrow, the foreman's instinct told him, Paul Bunyan would be roaring for them to quit the pasture and move the camp.

Hels Helson swung his shoulders for a heave on the halter rope, to take up the mile of slack. But it was the Blue Ox who took it up. The rope jerked violently in the Big Swede's stubborn grip. The next instant he was yanked so hard into the air that he soared toward the rising moon.

The Blue Ox had stolen just one glance over the valley's rim. It was enough to let him see the beaver jacks felling layer pines, and Pokemouche skidding logs. That last had instantaneously fired Babe with the fiercest jealous rage he had ever known. He saw nothing but red as he charged blindly into the valley, and all he thought about was how he would chew Pokemouche into beaver rags. Between blinks the Red Beaver saw the Blue Ox charging down, and he at once decided to do some rag-chewing on his own account.

Pokemouche did not lose his head. Instead, he stood on it, his all-powerful tail held aloft at ready. When Babe had charged within range, this tail with thunder in it fell like a bolt from the blue. The Blue Ox crashed to his knees. Soaring Hels Helson sailed over him and on. Now the Swede's grip was torn at last from the halter rope, and he lit in a sprawl over the bank of layer pine logs. Fortunately for Hels, he lit with his hip pockets up. The wind was knocked out of him, and he was both dazed and dumfounded, but otherwise he was unharmed. Hels sprawled there on the log bank, head and feet down, hip pockets high.

A second thunderbolt from the Red Beaver's tail crashed down between Babe's horns. The Blue Ox sank another seven feet on his knees. The two licks had addled and damaged him mightily. Babe's right eye was closing. He could see but dimly from his left, for it was cloudy with hot tears of pain. The earth spun dizzily under his front knees and hind hoofs, and overhead the darkening sky crazily whirled. Babe was actually out on his hoofs. Only the unquenchable spirit of his fighting heart kept him up and drove him on.

For Babe did shiver up and stagger on. Ere Pokemouche could thunder down with a third tail-shot or change ends, the Blue Ox had come to grips with him. Powerful jaws closed about the Red Beaver's throat.

Babe's strength began to surge up again. Snarling furious moos, the Blue Ox shook the Red Beaver like nine thousand rats.

For just a moment Babe had the best of the battle. He was simply too shaken by the two blasting blows to maintain such a raging pace of battle. Pokemouche twisted and changed ends, and after the first thirty shakes from Babe's jaws he began to spit, hiss, yowl, and claw like mad. And he was mad, that Pokemouche. He was a forest fire wrapped in a beaver's hide, and he was ready to burn Babe up.

Knotting himself into a great red ball, Pokemouche then uncurled in a ferocious lunge. So he jerked his throat free from Babe's teeth. The Red Beaver rolled over once, then came up with his back arched, his tail swollen so enormously that it appeared to be round, while his fur bristled and shot sparks, and an unearthly squawl yowled from between his bared tusks. Babe snarled defiant moos and started another staggering attack. Pokemouche leaped above the charge and came down on the back of the Blue Ox. He stuck. Then, with claw and fang, he began to rake Babe from stem to stern.

It was too much for flesh and blood to bear. Yet Babe certainly would have borne it had the fight continued to be fair, falling in his tracks before admitting defeat to any beaver. But when his one swimming eye dimly glimpsed Joe Le Mufraw stumping and rumbling for him, swinging a peavey at his head, Babe gave up.

The Blue Ox reared and wheeled about. Thus the peavey blow fell on his tail. Babe thought his tail was broken there, and as his tail was his pride, his pride was broken too. Without more ado, Babe lit out for home. Pokemouche clung to him, still raking him down, until the Iron Mountains were passed. Then the Red Beaver swung off. Stopping every so often to lick his wounds and to howl out doleful moos at the moon, Babe laboriously made his way toward the nub of the Saginaw.

It was still the dark hour before dawn when Babe reached the junction of Lakes Huron and Michigan. He was still groggy and more than half blind, and it only seemed to him that the lake water was harder and rougher than usual as he crossed for camp. Babe had forgotten Bunyan Bridge. Actually he was not wading at all, but wabbling and staggering across Johnny Inkslinger's one famous creation.

The main bridge suffered no damage. But all the fancy curlicues and finishing touches of limber timber were wrecked in Babe's crossing. It seemed like a trifling accident, but it was truly a tremendous trifle. Paul Bunyan never dreamed it, but the fabric of his destiny depended on this thread.

Paul Bunyan awoke to the lusty beauty of an Indian summer dawn. Frost steamed from the first rays of sunrise. The air crackled and sparkled with the abundant vitality of the season. The turning leaves of the hardwoods circled the great camp with sumptuous splashes of blazing color. Chopping-weather. Time for a move. Logging could wait no longer. But the next move must be out of the Saginaw and into the waiting wilderness of the north and west.

"A move without men," said the boss logger to himself, his eyes grim before the beauty of the dawn. "This here's the day they head for the Big Onion and the Old Sawdust Pile. The spell of a royal lie takes 'em on. They'll wait a winter, they'll wait all year, never giving up the hope that good old times will come. I know men. Human nature, that's the trouble," was Paul Bunyan's bitter thought.

The day of parting dawned. The music of the breakfast gut hammer clanged through the sunrise light. The jacks heaved out of the shanties, springing along in the woodsmen's stride. Red-faced from cold scrubbings, lean in their middles, swaggering their shoulders, lustily snapping galluses with horny thumbs, all heaved on for their flapjacks.

"Something to the critters," mused the boss logger. "Something makes 'em seem like kin, in spite of all their cussed human nature. They've improved a lot in the old Saginaw. I hate to think of breaking new men in. Why, they won't even know how to stretch their legs proper after riding behind Babe, new men won't."

But he would have to get the new men first. Paul Bunyan dismally wondered what trick the royal gent had up his sleeve. He still could not figure which way to turn.

It was Babe the Blue Ox who began to show him now. Every dismal doubt was forgotten by Paul Bunyan as the stricken creature hobbled into camp. With one wrathful glance Paul took in Babe's swollen and drooling eyes, clawed hide, bumped head, and maimed tail. The poor ox held up a grievously gnawed leg for Paul Bunyan to see, at the same time sounding small, piteous, whimpering moos.

"Beaver bites, for all their size," growled the boss logger, the old fight blazing in his eyes. Then he glared at Babe's dragging tail. The marks of the blow that had maimed it were plain. "A peavey lick," Paul growled on. "And one that could of been hit by nobody but a hero. So the river rover is up to tricks, hey!" roared Paul Bunyan, jerking off his mackinaw and spitting on his hands. "He's asked for it, and he's going to get it there! For busting Babe's tail he's going to get himself took apart! Before the sun sets, Joe Le Mufraw is to be riven, sundered, and hewed up the middle of himself, by the sizzled hides of the old Shadrach, Meshach, and Abednego!"

Just then Johnny Inkslinger pranced up from his marred bridge. The timekeeper was indignant to the point of fussiness.

"The bridge, Mr. Bunyan!" shrilled Johnny. "All the curlicues, Mr. Bunyan—"

"Blast bridges!" interrupted Paul Bunyan, too wrathful to be kind. "Mind orders. You get forty-eleven pine trees down and hewed into splints for Babe's tail." Then he turned to the jacks, who were staring out from the cookhouse. "You choppers there! I got another day of duty for you now. Get a move on to help Johnny with his splints. And don't a man leave camp till I come back from taking me a hero apart!"

With that, Paul Bunyan heaved into a gallop and disappeared in a cloud of dust. The choppers hustled to mind orders.

"Sounds like the old Saginaw again," they said.

Somehow their hearts were thumping as they had

never thumped from thoughts of the famous year to come.

Joe Le Mufraw had been dozing through the night, for the first time in his memory entirely failing to sleep like a log. He knew too well what the morning would bring. Paul Bunyan and battle. Nothing else. At last the river rover was certain that he wanted anything else. He had indeed overreached himself, or rather the Red Beaver had done that for him. Joe Le Mufraw's only hope was that he might arrange a treaty of peace through Hels Helson.

The dazed and dumbfounded Swede had finally fallen into slumber just as he lay on the log bank, head and feet down, hip pockets up. Three times during his troubled night the river rover rumbled terms of peace at the prone foreman, but Hels could not be roused. Joe Le Mufraw hoped to fare better with the dawn. All of his shagginess shivered with vain regret as he remembered the brutal peavey blow he had struck on the tail of the Blue Ox. But by dawn weariness overcame his fears, and he slept like a log at last.

At that hour the Red Beaver returned to camp. Pokemouche sat down near his master and friend and complacently licked his fur, yawning between licks, respectfully waiting for the river rover to awaken. Then his blinking gaze was caught by the Big Swede. Once more the tail of Pokemouche swelled and his fur bristled from an arching back. He rose silently into a crouch and crept forward, furtively stalking Hels Helson.

Neither Joe Le Mufraw nor the intended prey dreamed of what threatened. Slowly and softly Poke-mouche crept on velvet paws, stopping now and again to crouch down, a fierce mutter sounding from his throat. Then Pokemouche would slowly rise, craning his neck and peering with wide-eyed hunger at Hels Helson's hip pockets, and so continue his sinister advance.

The actual attack was in startling contrast to this slow and solemn preliminary. A scant hundred yards from the log bank the Red Beaver leaped. His sinuous body twisted in mid air, he elevated his tail at the same time, and then Pokemouche thudded down on his head. He stood on his head there, in perfect batting position. The tail swept over and down. The ensuing lick re-sounded like a shot from all the thirty barrels of Paul Bunyan's scatter cannon.

But Pokemouche had not intended this tail-shot to be a finishing one. An instinct of cruelty in the Red Beaver impelled him to play with Hels Helson before making an end of him. So Pokemouche held his punch in making the first blow.

But it brought a bellow from Hels Helson neverthe-less.

"Halp har! Halp noo!"

Charging across from the northern nub of the Sagi-naw, Paul Bunyan heard the rolling echoes of that ago-nized roar. The boss logger humped down to his mightiest stride.

Joe Le Mufraw heaved up and rumbled for his great beaver, but he was too late. Pokemouche was now roll-ing the tail-shots over in violent volleys.

Between the resounding shots the Big Swede vainly tried to rise or roll off the log bank. Every attempt was a vain one, because Pokemouche was whacking and paddling too fast. Hels never had time to rise or roll more than nine or eleven feet before he would be knocked back into paddling position again.

The Red Beaver increased the force of his volleys as he felt his temper working up to a killing pitch.

Aproaching the Iron Mountains, Paul Bunyan could hear the blows. His beard shook with a groan, then drooped with despair. He was hearing murder over yonder, and he would be too late to stop it. The first of the seven valleys was yet afar. Then, suddenly, Paul Bunyan lost his stride. An explosive blast shook the earth under his pounding boots. By the time the boss logger had looked round and found his stride again, there was only silence from the north. A desperate hope glittered in Paul's eyes as he plunged on.

The boss logger had guessed truly. Naturally the perilous dry mineral in Hels Helson's hip pockets had not long been able to withstand the intense and rapid fire from the Red Beaver's tail. Both of the pockets shook like tremblers, then erupted with volcanic blasts. The exploding snoose flared with the force of a hurricane into the eyes, ears, noses, and mouths of Pokemouche and Joe Le Mufraw.

The river rover dropped as though topped by a giant sledge. The Red Beaver bounced into a ball and began to roll, spitting and yowling in a fit of fear, down the first valley of the Seven Mississippis. Hels Helson wabbled to his feet. Snoose was so natural to him that this explosion had simply sneezed him into shape. At last he had the strength and energy to start for home. He limped stiffly in both legs, and the wind blew freezingly through the vents left by the volcanic blasts, but Hels did not care. He was on his feet again, out of danger, and on his way back to Babe, his boss logger, and fresh condition powders.

The fight was all over when Paul Bunyan galloped over the valley rim in his longest strides. Snoose, the mighty mineral, the potent panacea, was actually the hero of the last big battle of the old Saginaw and its environs. Hels Helson was never done with boasting about it. The shanty boys were powerfully impressed. So a new battle and labor cry was invented for men of the woods.

"Give 'er snoose!" woodsmen roar to this day when either a fierce fight or a tough job is at hand. "Give 'er snoose!" they roar, remembering always the violent victory of the panacea over Joe Le Mufraw and Pokemouche the Red Beaver.

The great beaver never got over his fit of fear. He rolled, clawed, spat, and yowled in a frenzy until he reached the confluence of the Seven Mississippis, and then he frantically turned to covering his trail. With water the powerful Pokemouche covered his trail from the terrible Swede whose hip pockets exploded with such abandon when smitten with the mightiest weapon known to the Red Beaver. All day and all night and for two more nights and days Pokemouche labored, building the first and greatest beaver dam of history. At the end of that time the waters of the last and largest of the Great Lakes chain were rising behind the dam, and the Seven Mississippis were no more. The overworked rivers seemed to be glad of an excuse to die into a lake.

The Red Beaver fled on. Again he halted, once more to cover his trail, this time with the Lake of the Woods. Pokemouche never again came to rest. All over the north he fled with his fear, and so for the famous lakes of the North Woods thanks are due to Pokemouche. To this day little beavers build little dams in honor of their great hero.

Though the fight and the victory were not his, Paul Bunyan nevertheless kept his vow and took Joe Le Mufraw apart. After a tough tussle which knocked the bark off both of them, the river rover was separated with a splintering crash.

But Joe Le Mufraw was truly a tree of a man. Each of his parts grew again, even as riven pines sprout anew. Joe named his second part Pete, after the King of Europe. Together the twins went back to Joe's old job in life. On they roved, into the depths of the north.

The men sent over by King Pete followed the northern trails, vainly seeking their new boss. So the race of French river rovers got its start. Always new men of the tribe ask for Joe Le Mufraw. It is a custom of the North Woods.

"You know Joe Le Mufraw?" the new man will ask.

"Sure, I know," the old-timer always replies. "I know *two* Joe Le Mufraw. One he's name' Pete."

XVIII

THE YEAR OF THE GOOD
OLD TIMES

KING PETE had a plot up his royal sleeve. The revelation of the sinister fact was in a message to Joe Le Mufraw. A trusty carrier eagle bore it unerringly to the first valley of the Seven Mississippis. The lightning bird saw Paul Bunyan straddling the splintered and parted river rover there. He swooped without a question to the boss logger's shoulder, sank his claws in, and nestled down for a breathing-spell. All the carrier eagles liked Paul Bunyan. Had they known how to do it, they would have forged messages for him simply to get more chances to roost, ruffle their feathers, and purr on his hospitable shoulder.

Still smoking with fighting wrath, Paul Bunyan was setting himself on the mark to gallop down the Red Beaver's trail when the carrier eagle first swooped. He hitched up his galluses, took another roll in his sleeves, swabbed off the sweat of battle, pocketed his behemoth bandanna, and sprung his knees to charge. Then he felt an itching in his left shoulder. There was no mistaking that itch. Certainly a carrier eagle was sinking in his claws. Paul Bunyan's heart bounded with hope as he saw a roll of royal paper in the lightning bird's beak.

"So the Royal Gent has made up his mind about men, hey?" said Paul genially to the eagle. All his rage vanished before the prospect of a new crew of jacks coming over. "Let's read her here."

The carrier eagle freely yielded the message, and then, feeling his duty done, began to purr in drowsy contentment. Paul Bunyan innocently unrolled the paper, lifted his forefinger, and began to spell the message out. He did not suspect that his erstwhile employment agent might be having traffic with Joe Le Mufraw. Paul Bunyan would have been the last to read another hero's mail, unless he thought there was treachery and evil in it. The message seemed to be addressed to himself.

"To the Boss Logger of Real America," it started there.

"Up to his old royal tricks," Paul Bunyan innocently smiled. "Trying to flatter me up, His Nibs is."

The Bunyan forefinger painfully spelled on.

"Here's hoping you got your men safe and sound, Old Socks," the next words said.

Paul Bunyan frowned, partly from puzzlement and partly from resentment at the royal familiarity. Now his first doubts about the message arose. King Pete had learned long ago that Paul Bunyan was not a hero he could either flatter up or get familiar with. The boss logger's sagacity was taking alarm. It told him that was queer—King Pete sending over men without a word about it all summer and fall.

The boss logger sat down to ponder as he read the message on. His sagacity so possessed him now that, without realizing it, he sat on the sundered river rover. The Mufraw was already sprouting new life, but he did not let on. Both his parts bore the burden of Paul Bunyan without a murmur or a shiver.

His sagacity scenting a perfidious plot, Paul Bunyan spelled the entire message out with never a qualm of conscience.

This is how it read:

To the Boss Logger of Real America:
Here's hoping you got your men safe and sound, Old Socks. I'm all set myself. Here's how she lays. I'll land at the Old Sawdust Pile New Year's to start the Year of the Good Old Times. Got a gang of highbankers and gyps and gals who'll take P. B.'s jacks into camp. Then you know what. They go to work in the Saginaw snoose mines. I'll have 'em in the hole so deep they'll be years working it out. It's plain to see where P. B. will get off. I'm doing all this because I'm a friend of yours, Old Socks.
Yours truly,

Pete the First

His Nibs, the Royal Gent, King of Europe

Paul Bunyan's first impulse was to rise up and charge for Europe without more ado. But his sagacity was working with too much power. It kept him cooled down and sitting there on the riven river rover. He was pondering his deepest as the sun wheeled down the sky. Night fell. Thrice the sun rose and set, and in the next dawn Paul Bunyan saw his powerful problem at last in a clear light.

He spoke it out:

"It's all up to the men themselves," the boss logger gravely said. "No men could have Liberty and Freedom more than they got it now. I could put the old fear into 'em by showing 'em King Pete's plot, but I never want men that way. If they go on with me, it's got to be because they've lost so much of their cussed human nature in the old Saginaw that all they want is to get out the logs. They come with Free Will, I take 'em with all my heart," Paul Bunyan solemnly affirmed. "They go on swallowing that royal lie and end up as slaves in the snoose mines; that's their look-out. Me, I believe in Free Will," affirmed the boss logger.

That settled the man part of the problem. The snoose question had to be taken up next.

"I make a new camp to the west, and then I move the snoose arsenal out of the Saginaw," Paul Bunyan decided. "There's a plenty to last even Hels Helson a lifetime. His Nibs can mine the rest all he pleases."

But where get new jacks if his own men turned him down? That was the next question. Now Paul Bunyan began to look around for the men that Joe Le Mufraw was supposed to have. Instead, he saw beavers. Instantly Paul Bunyan took in the situation. He grimly smiled.

"So the river rover double-dealt the King," he said. "Serves His Nibs royal well right."

Then he fell silent. Paul Bunyan was seeing the answer to his future in the swarming beavers there.

Not once had the beavers of this first valley neglected their labor in the days just past. They would keep working as jacks until ordered to desist by Pokemouche or Joe Le Mufraw. The Red Beaver was far away, out of his mind, madly building dams to cover his trail with water. In this dawn the little beavers swarmed as usual from their lodges and went to work in the woods with a vim. Now Paul Bunyan was struck by the delightful lack of human nature in the beaver jacks.

Never in their labors did the beaver choppers stop to exchange gossip, borry chaws, hitch up galluses, lace boots, blow noses, scratch ribs, pick slivers, charm warts, peek at their turnips for the time, breathe deep, light pipes, gape at birds, thumb ax-blades, fiddle with buckles and buttons, think of something, cross their hearts, part their hair, pare corns, or to ask conundrums. The beaver jacks chopped trees, trimmed logs, and strictly attended to the business at hand as they worked. Above all, to Paul Bunyan's astonishment and pleasure, not one pair of beavers in the woods dropped work to argue politics or fight over religion. The boss logger could hardly believe his eyes and ears. He rubbed both, then looked and listened again. Still not a sign of human nature was manifested by the beaver jacks there.

Ever and anon the layer pines crashed in an unbroken roar. Now Paul Bunyan tested the beavers to see if they would take orders from him. He feared they might not recognize a new leader.

"All out of the woods!" roared Paul. "To your lodges there!"

The reformed beavers of the first Mississippi Valley had learned from Pokemouche that such orders were to be obeyed. As the roar boomed down the valley, the beavers stopped chopping and sat up on their tails, sniffing and blinking. Then the whole host paddled obediently out of the woods. They had no sooner entered their lodges than Paul Bunyan called them out to work again. Without a murmur of complaint, the good beavers again obeyed. Paul Bunyan chuckled with relief and hope. Men would have growled and grumbled their heads off at orders being reversed on them like that.

"Beavers for me!" exulted the boss logger. "They got hair on their chests, the old fight in their eyes, and everything else a jack needs! And they ain't got human nature, by the old apples of the Sin and Fall!"

And to this day, "He works like a beaver" is the highest praise a boss logger can speak about a woodsman.

Nevertheless, these busy and obedient jacks had some kind of lack. Paul Bunyan had to admit it, after his exultation had died down a mite. What the lack was he could not say. He only knew that beavers did not warm him up. Never could he feel that they were somehow kin to him. Here was a new band of bullies, a fine bunch of timber savages for him; yet the fact seemed to do him no good. The prospect of logging ahead looked as gloomy as ever. The boss logger's heart kept aching for the old times in the Saginaw.

"The only good old life for me!" he dismally sighed. "I know nothing like it will come again. Not without my old men it won't. There's a powerful mystery about my feelings here. I wonder just what the trouble is," Paul Bunyan sighed on.

His sighing wonder was ended by the need for action. The river was dying. Plainly it was passing away into a lake. Its waters were quietly rising over the banks. Once more Paul Bunyan ordered the beavers out of the woods. Then he started down the valley. The carrier eagle still clung to his shoulder, purring spasmodically as it was shaken by Paul's hustling stride.

Behind him the two Joe Le Mufraws—one named Pete—were left free to escape to the north.

At the confluence of the Seven Mississippis Paul Bunyan took one rapid survey of the Red Beaver's dam, and he saw that the day of the mighty rivers was done. Steadily the dead waters rose toward lake level over the layer pines. Paul suffered no pangs over losing the tough timber. He only hated to see the seven rivers go.

But there was no time for mourning. The sun was sinking along. Before the valleys were entirely flooded, the new jacks should be moved west. By nightfall the bunk shanties would be beaver lodges. Paul Bunyan grimly made up his mind to that and sealed his bargain.

Firm for the future, Paul Bunyan started home. Only modern boss loggers who have changed from men to machines in the woods may know what passed in the deeps of the hero's heart as he resolved to change from men to beavers there.

Paul Bunyan entered camp from the west. Not until he saw that it was deserted by all save Babe and the Big Swede did he realize that, despite his resolution, he had cherished a last secret hope for his men. Now it faded in the certainty that they had quit camp and headed down for the Old Sawdust Pile without even a single "So long" for him.

But he was as grimly resolute as ever when Babe

limped up, wagging a mended tail. The Blue Ox was in shape to move camp now. In a week he would likely be ready to log.

"That's our life, Babe," said Paul Bunyan solemnly. "Come to the yoke here. We rouse up Hels, round up Johnny from his bridge, cross over, pick up beavers, and then logging goes on. We won't mourn men, by the old silver cord and golden bowl!"

By sunset Paul Bunyan was ready to quit the Saginaw.

During the absence of their Big Feller the shanty boys had brought to pass the most patriotic event of logging history. Among modern woodsmen the bunkhouse cranks contend that a lingering sense of guilt was the source of the jacks' actions in the grand affair. The cranks point out that Paul's men had been so busy gabbing about the good old times to come that they forgot the Fourther July in their last Saginaw summer. But few others heed the cranks. The true belief is that the spirit of the country had at last begun to get in its finest work on the bully men from Europe. The Saginaw was the sum and center of all Real Americanism in the era of the boss logger of the North Woods. After so many seasons in the land, always breathing the spirit in, the bulliest men of Europe could not help growing more and more akin to Paul Bunyan, the Realest American of all time.

Now, at last, the old Saginaw was getting in its finest work of all.

Not a shanty boy consciously felt guilty about neglecting the Fourther July, and not a one dreamed that he was due to wax patriotic as the Big Feller's final order was obeyed, the last duty done. In two days Babe was splinted up and on the mend. In the next the jacks puttered and chored at patching, darning, and calk-sharpening. For all their mighty talk, and though they would have died before admitting it, the men hated to quit camp and go over the hump.

"We got all the time in the world," they muttered sheepishly. "We can't rush the Year. No use going off half cocked."

Even the optimists roared no more about the Year having maybe fifteen months and starting early.

But eventually turkeys were rolled. Nobody could see any reason for further delay. The men had owned Freedom and Liberty for a long time now, and they couldn't let them go to waste any longer. The boss choppers passed the word that the start should be made next morning, whether or not the Big Feller had come back. Not a man ventured a notion about backing out. Yet all looked glum. It was an eventide of dismal silence. All the jacks were brooding as they rolled into their blankets. Every man lay wide-eyed, wondering why the Year of the Good Old Times no longer looked so good to him here.

"Mebbe we'll see the Big Feller when he heaves down to haul snoose," muttered a choreboy in a dreamy doze.

"Shet up sech pious nonsense," growled a boss chopper. "If we do see him, it'll be as man to man. Don't fergit ye're free."

But the boss chopper's growl was not so hearty. The others heard its note of doubt. The jacks brooded on in the dismal darkness, wondering why Liberty and Freedom no longer seemed what they were cracked up to be.

It was a noisy night. With Babe doctored and mended and with first aid administered to Hels Helson, Johnny Inkslinger had cheerfully turned to the repair of Bunyan Bridge. All day he had labored with the limber timber, to put back the curlicues and finishing touches knocked down by Babe's dragging tail. Johnny worked on into the night. The timekeeper whistled as he toiled. At last he had a famous job to his credit. He, too, had left his mark on the Saginaw. As he whistled and worked, his mind began to conceive prodigious patriotic ceremonies for tomorrow.

"We'll have a silver-tongued oration," chanted Johnny Inkslinger, between whistles. "We'll drive a golden spike. We'll bust a bottle here. We'll cut a cord. We'll have a grand march over Bunyan Bridge while the horn toots and the banner waves!"

The chant of the timekeeper throbbed through the shanty rows. The jacks tossed in their blankets. For a while Johnny Inkslinger whistled at his work. Then his chant throbbed once more.

"We'll put up a monument," the groaning shanty boys heard. "We'll mark it with the history of the Saginaw in five hundred words. 'Here Paul Bunyan and his men tamed the Big Auger, logged its valley off, and crossed Round River, which flows no more. Here in the old Saginaw.' That's how the words'll start," chanted Johnny Inkslinger. "Snoose Mountain, the Big Onion, and the trotting trees—"

The jacks stuffed blankets in their ears, but they

could not muffle out the timekeeper's chant. It roared rapturously on through the night, with intervals of whistling, reciting the mighty Saginaw story. The men could not but listen. They had to live again their lusty logging days. Memories shadowed and smothered every ruddy vision of the Year of the Good Old Times.

At dawn the spirit of the Saginaw was getting in its finest work at last. Every man felt something new bulging his left ribs and lumping in his throat as he rolled out of his blankets. When the gut hammer clanged, the jacks surged forth in a style they had never shown before. All halted before the shanties, as Inkslinger's patriotic chant throbbed on from the nub. Every man stood as though spellbound, his chest bulging alarmingly, his right fist clenched over his heart, his left arm extended and its hand spread in a gesture of salute. For a long moment the men maintained that position, their glassy upturned eyes reflecting the rays of the sunrise.

The reflected rays flashed blindingly over the nub and struck Johnny Inkslinger, as he rose from his last finishing touch. The timekeeper started for camp at once, thinking only to procure the old Quebec horn for tooting and his banner for waving, never daring to hope that he would not have to perform his grand ceremonies alone.

Entering camp, Johnny Inkslinger stopped as though thunderstruck. The jacks were now all standing with bowed heads, while the boss choppers led them in the creed. A heartfelt rumble of response sounded from each bully throat.

"My timber country!" The mighty words rumbled in solemn and dreadful tones. "May she always be right," spake the boss choppers. "May she always be right," sounded the reverent response. "But right or wrong." "Right or wrong." "My timber country!"

As the camp resounded with the last response, Johnny Inkslinger ecstatically seized the Quebec fish-horn and blew an ear-splitting toot. In the next instant he was shaking his banner in a hair-raising wave. The time-keeper choked with unspeakable emotion as he saw the men soulfully fall into a line of march. Certainly the spirit of the Saginaw was working with incredible power. It was even making the bulliest forget his breakfast flap-jacks.

Not a man fell out as the procession went on to the Saginaw end of Bunyan Bridge. Not a whisper of inter-ruption was heard as Johnny Inkslinger heaved for three hours in a silver-tongued opening address. At its end every jack's left ribs were bulging more than ever, and every one had a neck swelling over his mackinaw col-lar.

The ceremonies proceeded with unimaginable fervor. No Fourther July celebrated in the Saginaw could hold a candle to this day for patriotism. The veterans relived all the seasons of getting out the logs, and all were gloried up. Every hardship and danger was a fond mem-ory, as Inkslinger's silver tongue spieled on. The jacks even yearned for the skull-cracking blossoms of the posy hemlocks now.

At sunset the grand march was started for the north-ern shore. Nobody noticed that the Big Feller was mov-ing camp across the lake below the bridge. Not a man was feeling anything but the spirit of the old Saginaw.

Conflicting emotions stormed through Paul Bunyan's being as he saw his host of veterans marching over the bridge from the northern nub of the Saginaw. First he was simply pleased to think his jacks had owned the politeness not to quit him without a single so-long, after all. Next he was simply depressed at the prospect of parting ahead. Surely it had to be.

"Men," thought the boss logger mournfully. "You can't go against human nature. Even a hero can't."

But he would never parley or plead, Paul Bunyan inflexibly resolved. He would take just a minute to give a stump speech and wish the men well. Tell them they were his equals now, and not to forget it, as they had as much Freedom as himself. Maybe hint that he would see them as man to man when he made his trip to move the snoose arsenal up. But never let his kindness of heart go any further than that.

"Free Will," said Paul firmly. "Got to keep a grip on what I believe in."

So saying, he swung Babe and the camp into the plain north of the bridge. Then he waited for Johnny Inkslinger. The timekeeper marched up at attention. He clicked heels as he halted before Paul Bunyan, then fetched two fingers up smartly at salute.

"That's enough of flummery for a spell, Johnny," said Paul severely. "What's all the rest of this here about?"

The timekeeper was hoarsened by the day's orations, but he started another instantly. After the first few words Paul Bunyan's sagacity perceived that here was a triumph of patriotism. He marveled down at his men. What power could Johnny Inkslinger have worked on them that he himself did not know?

The jacks were out of the Saginaw now, and the spirit was leaving them. But enough remained to reveal something new and big about men to the Big Feller. Marveling down, Paul Bunyan was astounded to see that the left ribs of each jack were powerfully bulged and that his neck was swelled over his mackinaw collar by a lump in the man's throat. A formidable feeling entirely new to Paul Bunyan was inspired by the sight down there. It told him a truth his sagacity had searched for in vain. There they were, his old jacks of the Saginaw, the old fight in their eyes—but it was in their necks and left ribs that Paul Bunyan read the answer to the mystery which had baffled him always when he considered men.

Men also had the gift of kindness in their hearts!

"That's the answer there," said Paul Bunyan to himself, getting it pat. "Men. Hair on their chests, the old fight in their eyes, and also kindness in their hearts. That's what has bulged their ribs and swelled their necks at last! And that, by the old jubilee of Jerusalem, is what makes men kin to me!"

Now Paul Bunyan looked on his men as Real Americans, hearts, souls, and hides. As such they demanded a higher duty from him than simple use as jacks to get out the logs. A hero with kindness in his heart could get along fine with Freedom and Liberty because of the might of his arm and his sagacity. But men were not so mighty and wise.

"The royal gent would see their soft side and start working on it in no time," Paul Bunyan reflected. "As bullies of Europe they ran wild on His Nibs. But as Real Americans who learnt their kindness in the old Saginaw they would let him soft-soap 'em just like Johnny did. Slaves in the snoose mines," thought the Big Feller, shaking his head. "That's how their Year of the Good Old Times would surely end. No more Free Will. I'm protecting my kin."

He saw the way to do it there. The jacks were rapidly changing back into the bullies Paul was used to. Streaks of human nature were showing all through the host. Chaws were being borried, rib-scratching started up, turnips were peeked at, a bunch of swampers were charming warts, and political arguments began to roar. His beard concealing a fondly knowing smile, Paul Bunyan took the stump. That meant an old-time speech was due. The jacks stared up in silence.

"Just taking the old stump to say a so-long, men," said Paul Bunyan simply. "I'd stop here till morning, but I got to move on to the Seven Mississippis and pick up my new jacks there. So here's a short so-long, and I wish you all well."

He waited. Kindness swelled in the boss logger's own heart as he watched the men shuffle round and blink uneasily at each other. In the moment Paul Bunyan wondered if he knew men and their human nature so mightily, after all.

Soon his wonder was ended. The boss choppers stepped forward.

"Pickin' up yer new jacks, you say?" they roared up at him. "Who'll yer new jacks be, Big Feller?"

There was a terrific second of silence. Then:

"Beavers," said Paul Bunyan. "Just beavers, men."

For a moment the fading glow of the setting sun shone on a scene of profound quiet. The shanty boys stood as though petrified; then expressions of powerful emotions began to sweep swiftly over their rough faces. Angry astonishment, wrathful shame, raging resentment, murderous jealousy—these and kindred emotions were violently mirrored there. Then an expression of reckless resolution bristled from every countenance. So glowering and glaring, the men needed no words to declare their singleness of purpose.

As one man the host of jacks turned for Bunyan Bridge. They swept for it in a surging mass, seizing up dry grass and bush as they heaved on. Flints flashed in the gathering shadows. Tongues of fire leaped from innumerable torches. The flames converged in one vast blaze.

"Bunyan Bridge is burning down!" Johnny Inkslinger suddenly shrilled. "The men are burning the bridge behind them there!"

Paul Bunyan dropped a consoling hand on the timekeeper's shoulder, at the same time heaving an immense sigh of relief. He wondered no more. Certainly he had proved that he knew men, in, out, and all over.

"Never mind, Johnny," said Paul Bunyan kindly. "The jacks are inventing us a grand ceremony. Forevermore men will burn their bridges behind them when they go from one timber country to another. And you're the one who'll get a big name out of it."

The timekeeper was instantly consoled. Nothing could cheer him like the invention of a new ceremony.

The boss logger had one more chore to perform. The carrier eagle yet roosted on his shoulder. Paul at once rigged up a message for the lightning bird to tote back to the King of Europe. This was the message given to the eagle's care:

To Pete the First
His Nibs, the Royal Gent, King of Europe
Dear Sir:
   News that you figure on horning in here is to hand. Here's the latest from the Saginaw. Shot Gunderson has slayed and slaughtered himself, Squatter John is plastered with seventy-nine (79) mortgages, and Joe Le Mufraw is took apart. Enough said. Think it over.
                    Yours truly,
                       Plain Paul Bunyan
                          Just a Real American, that's all

Having burned their bridge behind them, the jacks piled into the shanties. Paul Bunyan watched until the last door was bolted. He felt no qualms of conscience over using the bully spirit of his men to suppress the kindness in their hearts. His own left ribs were sinking in. It was the boss logger of the North Woods who yayed Babe on for the waiting wilderness of the West.

Just once the great right hand of Paul Bunyan was raised in a rugged wave of farewell to the old Saginaw. He did not look back. Hels Helson as sturdily tramped by the side of the Blue Ox. The red flare from the burning bridge revealed the Big Swede's legs moving in their best bow-legged style, while his left paw nursed a barrel of fresh snoose and the right primed his cheek with a potent charge. Johnny Inkslinger turned for one salute, then marched at attention, his fingers stiff by his breeches seams.

The jacks bounced in their bunks as Babe speeded up. They grinned hugely to show they did not mind. Every bully had but one proud thought. The bunk shanties should never be beaver lodges now.

The last flicker of red from the burning bridge fell below the horizon.

"So long, old Saginaw," a boss chopper said. "There was never a better land for loggin' while she had it."

The night deepened. It was the end.